Inspired Living

Scott Maderer's *Inspired Living* is a masterful exploration of self-improvement and the power of enriching relationships. His insights on personal growth, leadership, and the profound impact we have on others echo the core values of mental fitness and social connectedness. It is essential reading for those on a journey to a purposeful, impactful life.

— **Alan Cox**, founder of EverYellow

Inspired Living is a beautiful reminder that true wealth lies not only in material possessions but also in the richness of our relationships and the impact we make in the lives of others. If you achieve financial success and it's lonely, you got there the wrong way.

—**Dan Miller**, *New York Times* best-selling author of *48 Days to the Work (and Life) You Love* and host of the *48 Days Podcast*

In *Inspired Living*, discover the magnetic pull of purpose, a compass guiding you to a life of unparalleled fulfillment. As each page unfolds, you'll find yourself immersed in a profound journey that beckons the soul to its truest calling. This isn't just a book—it's an awakening. Embrace it, and watch everything fall magically into place. A transformative must-read for those hungry for a life rich with meaning and intent!

—**Aaron T Walker**, founder of View from the Top

God created each one of us with a purpose. We're called to find joy and peace through Him, but we steer off track trying to do it our way. In *Inspired Living*, Scott describes how living every day with a stewardship mindset puts you right back where you need to be. Sharing your skills and your gifts with others is the key to unlocking your true calling. Allow Scott to guide you through this process and inspire you to find your true fulfillment

—**Marc Hall**, Certified Kingdom Advisor® and author of *Pursuing Spiritual Wealth: 40 Principles That Make Your Life Richer*

In *Inspired Living*, Scott presents a simple (though not easy) process that anyone can use to transform their life and begin to put together the puzzle of their call. This book will help anyone, regardless of age or background, begin to answer the question, "What do I want to be when I grow up?"

—**Kim Avery**, author of *The Prayer Powered Entrepreneur*

Inspired Living guides readers toward a purpose-driven and mindful life, offering wisdom and tools to cultivate a meaningful and fulfilling existence. Scott encourages individuals to find their passion, live with intention, and create a life that aligns with their values and desires. Many books try to give a one-size-fits-all formula. Scott presents multiple ways to identify your calling and take tangible steps to fulfill it. If you're serious about your purpose in life, you will certainly find a strategy that works for you!

—**Clint Hatton**, founder of BigBoldBrave, author of *Big Bold Brave: How to Live Courageously in a Risky World*

Inspired Living is like a masterclass in how to get to where you want to be in life. Scott's relatable style makes it easy to understand and apply the principles within. This book will help you clearly see the picture, recognize the pieces, and understand the process needed to complete the puzzle and bring your desired vision to reality.

—**Chris Rollins**, president of Rollins Performance Group, Inc.

Scott masterfully combines faith, purpose, and practicality to help you discover and fulfill your God-given calling with a clear road map. He guides you through the process of investing in yourself, nurturing your talents, and aligning your treasures with your purpose. So, if you want to make meaningful changes in your life and increase your ability to impact the world, then I highly recommend this book.

—**Bob Lotich**, author of *Simple Money, Rich Life*

I have often felt Scott is the yin to my yang. His systematic approach gave credibility and focus to my wandering creative thinking, but in *Inspired Living*, I found a curated understanding of how to become your best self, filled with creative language and beautifully told stories. If you want to change your life and believe that with the right steps, it's possible, Scott has given us the steps and encouragement to take the journey to become the best we can be. As I read *Inspired Living*, I took a highlighter to stay focused. Unfortunately, within the first few pages, I realized the density of life-changing thoughts made the portions left *unmarked* stand out too much. Finally, the practical exercises open the door for anyone to take this journey. Thanks for writing it, Scott.

—**Dow Tippett**, author of *7 Daily Choices*

I've had the privilege of seeing Scott coach others in real-time within the mastermind groups we've been a part of together. Scott is a master at getting to the heart of an issue and guiding others on their path to self-discovery. That he has decided to share his wisdom and experiences in *Inspired Living* means everyone can benefit from his years of hard-won knowledge.

—**Jeff Brown**, author of *Read to Lead* and host of the Read to Lead Podcast

Inspired Living

Assemble the Puzzle of Your Calling by Mastering
Your Time, Your Talent, and Your Treasures

C. Scott Maderer

NEW YORK

LONDON • NASHVILLE • MELBOURNE • VANCOUVER

Inspired Living

Assemble the Puzzle of Your Calling by Mastering Your Time, Your Talent, and Your Treasures

© 2024 C. Scott Maderer

Published in New York, New York, by Morgan James Publishing. Morgan James is a trademark of Morgan James, LLC. www.MorganJamesPublishing.com

Proudly distributed by Publishers Group West®

A **FREE** ebook edition is available for you or a friend with the purchase of this print book.

CLEARLY SIGN YOUR NAME ABOVE

Instructions to claim your free ebook edition:
1. Visit MorganJamesBOGO.com
2. Sign your name CLEARLY in the space above
3. Complete the form and submit a photo of this entire page
4. You or your friend can download the ebook to your preferred device

ISBN 9781636983400 paperback
ISBN 9781636983417 ebook
Library of Congress Control Number:
2023947063

Cover and Interior Design by:
Chris Treccani
www.3dogcreative.net

Morgan James is a proud partner of Habitat for Humanity Peninsula and Greater Williamsburg. Partners in building since 2006.

Get involved today! Visit: www.morgan-james-publishing.com/giving-back

To my wife, son, bonus daughter, and two goddaughters.
You are the reason I do everything I do.

Table of Contents

Foreword by Dan Miller

We live in a world that is constantly moving, filled with an endless stream of responsibilities, expectations, and distractions. Amid the chaos, it's easy to lose sight of what truly matters and find ourselves swept away in the currents of everyday life. But what if there was a way to navigate these waters with purpose and intention? What if we could find the key to living a life that is truly inspired?

In *Inspired Living*, Scott Maderer invites us on a transformative journey to unlock our full potential and embrace a life of purpose, abundance, and fulfillment. Drawing upon his deep well of wisdom and personal coaching experiences, Scott masterfully guides us through a tapestry of concepts that, when woven together, form the very fabric of a life well lived.

At the heart of this book lies the belief that to truly live an inspired life, we must first embark upon the journey of self-discovery. Scott reminds us of the profound importance of knowing ourselves—the good, the bad, and everything in between. It's in this self-awareness that we begin to uncover our passions, values, and unique strengths. Armed with this knowledge, we can then invest in ourselves, nurturing our growth and continually striving to become the best versions of ourselves.

But Scott doesn't stop there. He eloquently emphasizes the significance of investing in others—the act of extending a helping hand, offering support, and building meaningful connections. By fostering a mindset of abundance, we open ourselves up to the transformative power of generosity and compassion. Scott reminds us that true wealth lies not only in material possessions but also in the richness of our relationships and the impact we make on the lives of others.

As we move through the pages of this book, Scott deftly guides us toward developing our influence and cultivating leadership skills. He underscores the notion that leadership is not confined to a title or position but is a way of being—a conscious choice to inspire and empower those around us. Through intentional habits, we learn to shape our days with purpose and discipline, embracing the slow and steady progress that ultimately leads to significant transformation. Scott's insights remind us that true growth lies not in drastic overnight changes but in the commitment to getting just 1 percent better each day.

One of the most profound aspects of *Inspired Living* is its emphasis on discovering our purpose and calling—the very essence of our existence. Scott reminds us of "Ikigai," the Japanese term for finding one's reason for being. With great care and wisdom, he helps us unravel the intricate layers of our lives, exploring the intersections of passion, mission, vocation, and profession. Through this process, we uncover the deep-rooted fulfillment that comes from aligning our actions with our purpose.

Throughout the book, Scott weaves a thread of stewardship—a call to earn, save, and give. He reminds us that life is not a solitary journey but a shared experience, and it is our responsibility to use our resources wisely, not just for our own benefit but for the betterment of the world around us. With poignant stories and practical guidance, he inspires us to embrace the interconnectedness of our lives and the profound impact we can make through our choices.

Finally, Scott poetically compares life to a puzzle, urging us to construct the edges before filling in the middle. In these words, we find solace and encouragement, knowing that life is a journey of gradual progression and continuous discovery. As we navigate the unknown, piece by piece, we realize that the beauty lies not only in the completed picture but in the process itself—the moments of growth, the setbacks, and the triumphs that shape us into who we are meant to be.

In *Inspired Living*, Scott Maderer has crafted a profound and inspiring guidebook for those seeking to live a life of purpose, abundance, and meaning. May we know ourselves, invest in ourselves and others, cultivate an abundance mindset, develop our influence, build intentional habits, and align our actions with our purpose. Through these principles, we discover the true essence of Inspired Living—a life lived with intention, fulfillment, and unwavering joy.

I am confident this book will inspire and empower you to embark on your own journey toward an inspired life.

—**Dan Miller,** *New York Times* best-selling author of *48 Days to the Work (and Life) You Love* and host of the *48 Days Podcast*

Introduction

True Change Is Painful yet Possible

. . . .

Why did you pick up this book?
For many of you, it's because you're ready to make a significant change in your life. This typically comes after waking up and realizing that something has to give.

So many of us go day-to-day with an existential crisis building up inside of us like a dormant volcano. A maelstrom of emotions hides under the surface—hot lava, volcanic ash, and gases fume in a metaphorical magma chamber where our hopes and dreams go to die.

Inevitably, the volcano erupts and leaves us in a tizzy. We have the heartbreaking epiphany that our life has been pretty plain and boring—or maybe exciting, but in all the wrong ways. We realize we've been operating on autopilot and without direction, leaving us painfully aware of how we never developed an influence, impacted the world, or excelled in some pursuit in our life that we're passionate about.

For some people, this eruption doesn't do much to light a fire within them. Believing themselves too far down the rabbit hole, they look back with regret and make excuses that help them feel better about themselves. Perhaps they look at all the money they've collected, ignoring the fact that they feel unfulfilled and lost in the maze of the rat race. Unfortunately, for these folks, the emotional lie will never be uncovered.

For others, this epiphany inspires them to make a major pivot. They don't feel comfortable living a life without a deeper purpose, and they launch into a soul-searching adventure. They may make a career change, start crossing items off their bucket lists, pick up helpful books (like this one, perhaps), or take some other measures to change the trajectory of their lives.

Unfortunately, even those efforts fall short. An enthusiastic launch into finding a life of meaning typically turns into a short-lived stint and back to normal in short order. An unsustainable approach or pace quickly unravels any real progress. They start with the right aim, but they don't follow through on the execution, or they take on too much at once and end up failing in their efforts.

Often, this comes from executing without taking a look at the big picture of what they're looking to achieve. They're told by some supposed "expert" to follow ten specific steps, so they blindly follow those ten specific steps as if they're a one-size-fits-all program that works for everyone. They dive headfirst into a process, frantically trying to complete the puzzle without looking at the box to know what the result is supposed to even look like.

Their futile attempt leads to more discouragement and despair, creating a vicious cycle where they think living out a life of meaning is nothing but a pipe dream.

Others don't necessarily need the eruption in order to decide to make a significant change. Maybe you're fresh out of high school or college, wondering what to do with your life. Perhaps you found yourself running on autopilot, and something snapped you out of it. Heck, maybe you came across some of my content online, or heard me on a podcast, and decided you wanted to learn more.

Regardless, the fact you're holding this book tells me you have a desire to discover and live out your unique calling. You want something achievable and sustainable. You're willing to invest your time and a few bucks in this book to take action. And you're willing to deal with the discomfort that comes with meaningful change.

> Change happens when the pain of staying the same
> is greater than the pain of change.
> **—Tony Robbins**

If you aren't yet living your calling, operating in this world as your truest and best self, in some way, you're living a lie. If that sounds harsh, it's because it is a little harsh. There's no judgment in there, though. That's not for me to do. It's just a matter of fact. If you're not living as your truest or best self, some part of what you're doing is inauthentic. There's a gap between your authentic self and how you're living your life today. By definition. My goal is for you to have begun closing that gap by the time you close this book. That's my singular goal for the relationship we began building when you started reading.

To help, I'm going to help you identify what exactly it is to be operating in this world as your truest and best self, in every part of your life. I'll help you pursue a skill, passion, or area of knowledge in your life so you can make it play a larger role in your bigger picture. And I'll help you incorporate that into every aspect of your life so you can be the same authentic person at home as you are at work, in your community, and everywhere else you go.

And, finally, I'm going to help you create a legacy and live a life of meaning, impact, and fulfillment that lasts far longer than your earthly body does.

Everyone Has a Puzzle to Build

I like to think of life as a puzzle, of sorts. Our lives are full of pieces, some interconnected, others seemingly miles apart. Fully assembled, however, all the pieces point to a single picture of who we are, what we do, and what matters most to us.

Unlike the typical jigsaw puzzle, our puzzle does not come with a static image. We're not told what our puzzle needs to look like assembled. We can choose what our picture looks like on the outside of the box. And, for many people reading this book, it's likely that the image currently on the outside of your box will be different from the one you envision at the end of the book.

How? Because images are a snapshot. The image on the outside of your box might look breathtaking. Or it might look like someone spilled five puzzles on the floor, and you have parts of one interconnected with parts of another in a way that doesn't make any sense.

I have no idea. But what I can promise you is by the end of the book, you will design a puzzle that paints the picture of a life you love and have all the pieces necessary to assemble it.

Find Your Comfort

As I've navigated my great puzzle of life, I've always looked to faith to find comfort. Of course, that doesn't mean I have life figured out entirely—no one does. That's part of the beauty of life. We design our puzzle and then learn and grow as we're assembling it. Sometimes, we continue to tweak our picture, adding or removing features we believe will result in our getting closer to our ideal puzzle as we learn more about ourselves.

However, just because we won't always know exactly what our puzzle is going to look like, I've developed a deep-seated belief that God knows exactly what our puzzle will look like when we're living out our calling. He reveals it to us slowly, through a series of life and learning events, some more challenging than others. But he has blessed every one of us with a true "calling" in life, the ideal masterpiece he created for us that we can all build toward if we pursue it with great intentionality.

The problem? While we all have a calling, so few of us really believe we can get there.

> The mass of men lead lives of quiet desperation.
> **–Henry David Thoreau**

In the context of this book, I'll walk you through a process I use in my personal life and with my coaching clients all around the world to help discover the puzzle God designed for each of us.

Like a jigsaw puzzle, we'll go one step at a time, systematically working to identify the image, find the right pieces, assemble them in a simple, logical order, and evaluate whether we're on the right track or need to adjust along the way.

Having gone through this process hundreds, if not thousands, of times with people from all walks of life, I understand you might have some doubts. Perhaps you doubt something about yourself, whether you do have a true calling, or whether you did have a true calling but somehow "missed it." Or perhaps you might be confident that you have a true calling but feel stuck because of life circumstances: a busy job, tight finances, or some other external limitation. Or maybe you question whether this whole concept of a "calling" even exists.

If any of those feel familiar to you, it's natural. I've worked with everyone from corporate executives to single parents. Everyone comes in with some questions, about themselves, their circumstances, or the whole concept itself. That's natural, and I don't try to convince you that those feelings are wrong. Instead, I'm going to ask you to temporarily find comfort in the fact that you're not alone in those feelings, and the process you're about to go through is the exact same process each of those people did to build a better, more fulfilling life.

You do have a calling. You can start working toward it no matter what your circumstances. And you can build a life you love. All you have to do is take a series of small steps forward that I'll walk you through over the next chapters.

The truth is, the difference between achieving the life you want to live versus looking back in regret later comes down to how much you want it. You can either pursue your calling or perceive it as a pipe dream and let it never come to fruition.

Without completing your puzzle, you'll find yourself stuck living day-to-day in a human beehive. Work your nine-to-five, get home, and perform the same routine—dinner, put the kids to bed, Netflix, rinse, and repeat. When your golden years of retirement finally roll around, you can look back at how much you've advanced in your career.

It feels nice to enjoy the trappings of success and excel in your career, but don't you think it's better to do that while leaving a legacy? Don't you think it's better to impact the world, change the lives of others, and operate in a zone where your God-given talents are put to good use—to live out your calling? Instead of simply waiting for retirement, you come alive now.

You Might Be Thinking . . .

At this point, you might be thinking that I seem like one of those many "gurus" out there who think they have a "simple fix" or clear-cut equation. You might wonder whether I'm another one of those phonies with a made-up formula for achieving a life of personal and financial freedom. Or that I just tout a different iteration of the same junk "systems" people peddle to help you change your life in a weekend.

Well, I have good news for you: What I do is simple. But it's not some "change your life in a weekend" promise where I convince you I have everything figured out, and you will too if you throw a bunch of money at me. In fact, some of my most successful coaching clients are the ones who have paid me the least. I don't hide results behind promises that if you just hire me for my "Platinum Coaching Accelerator" your problems will be solved. You can do everything you need to do to change your life by slowly working through this book.

To be fair, what many of those gurus say isn't always a load of baloney. But there's definitely a lot of baloney out there. The truth is, however, when it comes to achieving the life of your dreams, it's a process, not an event. It's a multifaceted, interconnected series of habits and frameworks that'll work in tandem, with plenty of loops within each intentional series of events.

So, I treat my framework just like that: a series of simple, interconnected processes that take thinking, planning, and good old hard work to achieve. But anyone can do it.

If you opened this book looking for a quick fix, you came to the wrong place. But if you want life-tested habits and frameworks to identify your calling and live it out, we're in business.

Will you join me on this journey?

Over the next three parts, I'll walk you through what helped me—and plenty of others—build their puzzle.

1. The Picture: How to Live Out Your Calling
2. The Pieces: The "Loops and Sockets" Needed to Live Out Your Calling
3. The Process: How to Complete the Puzzle and Achieve Your Calling

Let's do it.

Part 1:

The Picture: How to Live Out Your Calling

L et me share with you the reason that 95 percent of self-help journeys fail, and why we keep going back to the shelves hoping the next book will provide the answer. It's because we look for tools and techniques first. We demand that the author or motivational speaker simply show us what to do. We think that will be enough.

When we read a few of the chapters and put their strategies into place, things seem to go well—for a while. Then, we find that our life hasn't actually changed from the ground up. In other words, we've just applied new paint to a house with a crumbling foundation. When we begin to feel the strain of this deep disorder, we go hunting for fresh tools and techniques.

In truth, the answer lies in the foundation. But fixing a foundation is much more difficult, time-consuming, and expensive than throwing on new paint. Instead of buying another book or attending another seminar, you have to face the beliefs, mindsets, and attitudes you possess that get you the results you have. The truth is ugly. Even admitting that we just might be our own worst enemy, or that we don't actually believe we have a purpose, is tough. It's much easier to keep things surface-level.

If you want to discover and live out your calling, it must start with doing the deep work. You must invest in yourself, identifying and correcting limiting beliefs. You've got to reorient your mindset, which mostly has to do with what you allow yourself to see or hear. Are you ready to make significant changes to your media and information diet? Most people are not. You need to learn what and how to feed your body, mind, and soul, and rebuild your habits from the ground up.

From there, you take a look outside yourself. You invest in others, even if you feel more like Ebenezer Scrooge than Mr. Rogers on the inside. Put differently, you stop being so wrapped up in yourself and help others in any way you can. This process shows you deep passions that will motivate you to get out of bed in the morning. These are the first inklings on the way to discovering your calling. You begin to develop a true influence and impact, starting infinitesimally small and then radiating outward to the world—and every single step is racked with pain and difficulty.

It doesn't come overnight. It doesn't come easily. You have to learn to flex your "no" muscle, falling in love with delayed gratification. However, over time, you begin to realize something: There might actually be a very good reason you were placed on this earth. You might actually have a calling.

Want to discover it? I invite you to start digging with me, to the very foundation. It won't be easy, but it will be worth it.

We will break down discovering your calling and laying a lasting foundation into four chapters:

- Invest in Yourself
- Invest in Others
- Develop Your Influence
- Impact the World

Chapter 1:

Invest in Yourself

· · · · · · · · · · · · ·

Faltering profit margins. Living in constant fear of losing yet another client. Feeling like an imposter. Stuck in a cycle where you don't have time to do everything you want to do. Hunkering down in survival mode, prioritizing the "important" stuff, and leaving your calling on hold.

Three years ago, those descriptions matched Peder perfectly.

At the time, Peder's business was struggling, and he genuinely considered shutting it down. What was once a rocket launch of a business idea was now in a phase that my middle school science students would have called "spaghettification." If you don't speak geek, it just means Peder's initial burst of enthusiasm was now draining into a black hole of crushed aspirations and financial woes.

In plain English, Peder began to lose hope. He wanted to reinvigorate his business; he wanted to keep working toward making the impact he was trying to make. And while Peder did plenty, he didn't do the right things.

Peder and Alison Aadahl 1: How It Started

We were approaching our ten-year anniversary mark and wanted to improve our marriage, especially since many couples get divorced around this time. I remember us having the realization of "Oh, we can't do this by ourselves. We need outside help." Sometimes you need someone to help you see the forest through the trees.

Since working with Scott, we have realized that comparison doesn't accomplish anything. It's easy to think, "My grocery bill is too high, I bet other people spend less." But here's the thing: most people probably don't even know what they spend! Above all, you have to invest in yourself to get the results you want.

Limiting Beliefs Will Take the Wind Out of Your Sails

> There was a moment where we realized that if we don't get outside help, our situation will only get worse and get worse faster. Knowing that, we realized we couldn't do it on our own and needed outside help.
>
> —Peder Aadahl

Peder's actions led him to the pickle he was in, but those actions ran deeper than making repeated errors or sporting a poor business model. Peder's situation was the culmination of a scarcity mentality; the limiting beliefs dictating his life sabotaged his behavior, habits, actions, and, ultimately, his results.

Limiting beliefs are those beliefs about ourselves that creep up and hold us back. We often hold limiting beliefs subconsciously, unaware of how they're constantly undermining our confidence. They're a quiet devil sitting on our shoulders, telling us we're going to fail or that we can't succeed. They're the biggest antagonist we'll ever face—our inner critic—who holds us back from becoming and being our best selves.

Many times, limiting beliefs lead to self-fulfilling prophecies. The moment you believe you can't do something is the moment you've set yourself up for failure. Maybe you believe you're not anything special. Perhaps you believe the competition is too fierce to make it in your respective industry. The fact is, every human has limiting beliefs, and they come in many different forms.

Wearing the "Superhero Cape" Can Weigh You Down

> The greatest thing that happened in my career
> when I turned thirty-seven was hiring an assistant.
> **—Peder Aadahl**

For many of my clients, their limiting beliefs stem from setting the bar too high. They race around trying to be perfect, trying to be the superhero, or having to be the one that solves every problem. When they can't solve every problem, they end up feeling worse about themselves.

I urge you to begin investing in yourself by recognizing and reaffirming your self-worth, before shooting yourself down for not being worth more. There are things you are good at—that's how you got to where you are—and that's more than enough. You're already a superhero in your own right; there's no need to people-please. Celebrate your successes; cultivate compassion for the hard. Picking up and reading this book is a show in itself of how committed you are to growing and becoming the best version of yourself.

So, I urge you to ditch all the pressure that comes with wearing that "superhero cape." Start understanding your skills, abilities, strengths, and even your weaknesses (we'll get to this in a bit). Realize that it's not about knowing everything, and it's not about being perfect. If you hold unrealistic expectations for yourself, you set yourself up for disappointment—we're all human, after all.

Be logical, get pragmatic, accept yourself for who you are, and only aspire to do what you're comfortable doing. If you're having trouble doing that, you'll need to start taking further measures to shut your inner critic up and effectively silence the limiting beliefs holding you back.

Silence Your Inner Critic

When I met Peder, he was stuck in his own head. Instead of setting his sights on the finish line, he was trying not to trip on the ground in front of his feet.

An inner critic dominated his thoughts, giving a louder voice to his shortcomings than his ambitions. Whether he attributed his failures to bad luck or let his frustrations tear down his self-esteem, his inner critic got in the way of his success.

Peder's wife, Alison, even tried to help. An extra set of hands didn't prove fruitful, however, and instead marked a last-ditch effort that ended up stressing both of them out. Alison worked her tail off night and day, putting in overtime hours, trying all she could to help her husband bounce his business back—to no avail.

Finally, with nowhere to turn to, Peder hired me. With that decision, Peder took a pivotal step toward investing in himself. He started to dig himself out of his rut by seeking someone who knew how to shut that inner critic up.

Don't Fall Victim to the "3 Ps" of Beliefs

If you always think you'll fail, you will fail. If you believe you aren't good enough, you aren't. It's as simple as that. As long as you believe you're stuck, you're stuck.

Peder believed his shortcomings were personal, permanent, and pervasive. So many of my clients are in the same boat when they hire me, to the point that I've now titled these beliefs as the "3 Ps."

Perhaps you currently live in a 3 P state of mind without even knowing it. For example, do these phrases sound familiar?

- "It's me; I'm the problem."
- "It's always been this way."
- "It's in every component of my life."

When Peder brought me on, I helped him attack those fundamental limiting beliefs. I strived to make him feel more empowered and understand that he needed to take life by the reins and have some more faith in himself. With the changing of his belief system, his behavior and habits soon followed.

From there, the results started to appear. Fast-forward to the present. Peder and Alison have been enjoying the view from the top. They're six-figure earners who've changed their trajectory and achieved their calling, with no signs of slowing down their upward momentum. I didn't get them there; I just helped Peder realize he was getting in his own way—that he was acting as his own worst enemy.

Garbage In, Garbage Out

Admittedly, Peder's business didn't look too good when he hired me. I had to offer tons of advice between finances, positioning, pricing, and more—but it all came down to that same catalyst. Peder sabotaged himself by fueling poor behavior and habits with his limiting beliefs. Peder was immersed in a vicious cycle, capitulating losses and trying to plug holes in the hull of his boat instead of identifying the rocks poking holes in it.

When I teach my clients to invest in themselves, it starts by evaluating their current mentality. If they have a negative disposition that gives them unproductive thinking patterns, I coach them on reframing their mindset and dialing their thoughts to more positive frequencies. I help them shift their internal monologue from a broken 3 Ps record to developing habits that will either reinforce or reform their key strengths and weaknesses.

I do a specific exercise with clients every six months to ensure their limiting beliefs don't hold them back. It revolves around replacing limiting beliefs with "enabling truths," and it goes something like this:

- Take a few hours to brainstorm what limiting beliefs you hold about yourself. (What do you beat yourself up with? What negative statements do you make about your capacities?)
- Put a list of those limiting beliefs onto a sheet or an Excel document.
- Convert those limiting beliefs into enabling truths—an action you can take, a shift in your mindset, a reminder about past accomplishments, etc.
- Read *only* the enabling truths every day for six months, and then repeat the exercise.

Once limiting beliefs are replaced by enabling truths, your behaviors and habits will start aligning with the results you want. The shift in your mentality will create a ripple effect and that mental momentum will carry into every aspect of your life from the macro to the micro level.

Believe in Yourself

If you've ever heard of *Star Wars*, you've probably heard of Master Yoda. He has a cult classic quote: "Fear is the path to the dark side. Fear leads to anger. Anger leads to hate. Hate leads to suffering."

Why is this important? Well, I just wanted to give you a fair warning that I'm about to have a Master Yoda moment. *Star Wars* fan or not, I urge you to read this next section extra carefully.

Your feelings are caused by your thoughts. Your thoughts will dictate your actions. Your actions will manifest your results. Your results will either reinforce or disprove your initial thoughts. After proving yourself right or wrong over and over again, your thoughts will solidify as beliefs. Your beliefs will drive your behaviors and habits, which weigh on your entire picture from a macro to micro level.

If your behaviors and habits *don't* align with the results you want, you'll develop more limiting beliefs. If your behaviors and habits *do* align with the results you want, you'll begin silencing your inner critic.

Reread that last paragraph, a few times even. This is important because our behaviors and habits influence our beliefs. If we work hard but don't head in the direction we want, we can mistakenly believe there's something wrong with us. In that case, the truth is, there's nothing wrong with you; you just need to take different actions and form different habits to get on the path toward the results you want.

Investing in yourself and working toward your calling all starts with believing in yourself. You need to believe in yourself if you want the other pieces of the puzzle to fall into place.

Those who never learn to believe in themselves will perpetually find themselves stuck in a self-fulfilling prophecy until they break themselves out of it. Their poor behavior and habits compound, fueling their wavering self-esteem and further setting them up for overall failure.

> Belief creates action; action creates belief.
> —Scott Tandem

Unfortunately, getting your behaviors and habits to align with your desired results isn't as simple as redirecting negative thoughts and replacing your limiting beliefs with enabling truths. It requires hacking the "habit loop," which we'll get to in a moment. But, believe it or not, starting the process of hacking the habit loop is as simple as changing your mentality from "I can't do this" to "I *can* do this."

What Are You Feeding Your Body, Mind, and Soul With?

We can have the same external actions, but it's the character and our motivations behind those actions that underpin what we do and how we do it. That's why we need to bolster our thought space by extinguishing limiting beliefs and believing in ourselves.

If our mind is running on empty, it will feel more difficult to stay authentic and make big decisions. If your internal motivations and character are strong and centered around specific morals, however, taking the right action will become second nature.

Think about what you consume and how that might affect your thought space. If all you're eating is junk food, for example, you won't be physically healthy. How, then, do you expect to be mentally healthy? If all you're doing is binge-watching Netflix (and getting three hours of sleep every night as a result), how do you expect to perform at your full mental capacity?

Looking at your strengths is a great way to feel better about yourself, and they can serve as a reminder of your growth. But it's equally important to wrap your head around what you're not doing well with.

You need to answer to yourself and ask yourself the hard questions. What holds you back from getting to where you want to be? Who are you when nobody's around? What negative thoughts do you tell yourself? What stories are you imprinting? How are you making decisions? What's your motivation behind those decisions?

Reinforce Good Habits and Reform Bad Habits

I take set, structured times with my clients to examine habits as part of our quarterly and annual reviews. It's not something they need to do every day or every week, but they always have three to five habits that are manifesting the results they want.

Habits that give you the right results ought to be reinforced, while those that aren't serving you ought to be replaced. Additionally, those that disrupt your trajectory ought to be eliminated. It's about being intentional with homing in on the habits you want to keep and reforming the habits you want to change.

If you want to lose weight, for example, then a simple change in your habits can start a domino effect of differences. Maybe you stop grabbing that cookie when you go to the break room. Possibly you grab an apple instead, or take that time to go for a stroll around the building. After a week, you don't crave that cookie anymore. Your body has adjusted. The next step might be cutting out that bagel you always have for breakfast and substituting it with oatmeal. And so on.

Hack the Habit Loop

As I briefly alluded to earlier, reinforcing good habits and reforming bad habits can best be done by hacking the habit loop. Hacking the habit loop isn't about exercising willpower or putting your mind over matter. You can't just muscle through and force yourself to create a new habit or break an old one. Doing so requires a calculated, intentional process of dissecting your habit loop and reprogramming it in your favor.

Before we get into hacking the habit loop, you're probably wondering what, exactly, *is* the habit loop. The habit loop (identified by Charles Duhigg in *The Power of Habit*) looks something like this:

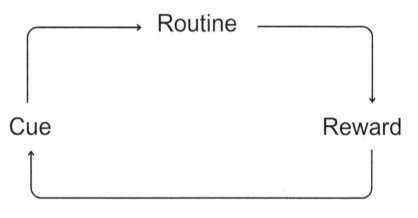

The Habit Loop

Building and breaking habits are similar, and hacking the habit loop goes like this:
1. Start with routine.
   a. Identify the routine that you want to break or start. It can be a bad habit you want to break or a new routine you want to create.
   b. It's often the easiest part of the habit to identify.
2. Then experiment with rewards.
   a. Rewards satisfy cravings—even unconscious ones.
   b. The reward may (or may not) be the result of the habit.

c. The reward can be internal or external.

d. To break a habit, replace the reward—don't remove it.

e. To create a new habit, you need a strong enough reward.

f. Examine the rewards and how you feel.

3. Isolate the cue.

a. This is the trigger.

b. It's typically the hardest part of the habit to identify.

c. Cues are usually something like location, time, emotional state, or other people that immediately precede the action.

4. Create a plan.

a. A habit is a choice that we make, then we stop thinking about it but continue doing it.

b. It saves energy to do this and rewards us.

c. To create or break a habit, have an implementation intention.

i. This has the form of "When X, I will Y and Z."

A common pitfall occurs when people make the false assumption that hacking the habit loop means implementing "perfect" habits day in and day out. In reality, it's more about implementing "keystone habits." Keystone habits are certain habits you've broken or adopted that produce a landslide of other positive changes. Examples include exercising regularly, sticking to a budget, eating family meals, making your bed every morning, keeping a food journal, keeping a gratitude journal, and so on.

Redirecting negative thoughts and replacing your limiting beliefs with enabling truths causes growth and abundance-based thinking. And while that behind-the-scenes work is a pivotal component in setting the aim of your overall trajectory, the inertia gets created with the actions you take. Taking the right action can only happen when your behaviors and habits align with your desired results, meaning you must master the art of hacking the habit loop.

Employ Habit Stacking

Beyond how I help people hack the habit loop, there's a popular method for adjusting your habits called "habit stacking." Habit stacking revolves around connecting new habits to existing ones. James Clear writes about this in his book, *Atomic Habits*.

Believe it or not, habit stacking works to rewire your brain for the better. I'm going to do some more geek speak here, so I apologize in advance if you want to hang me from the flagpole by my undergarments: Habit stacking is centered on "synaptic pruning." It sounds complex, but it's a pretty intuitive concept. The basic principle is a reinforcement of the notion that consistent practice keeps your skills sharp.

Synaptic pruning is a fancy way of saying that your brain discards connections between neurons when they don't get used but keeps them around and builds up the connections of habits we regularly perform. In other words, synapses that collect dust will get sent to the dump, while synapses that get used frequently will keep developing.

If you play guitar, for example, your brain will strengthen the connections between those musical neurons. Likewise, someone who isn't a guitar player isn't going to strengthen those connections in their brain. Because of synaptic pruning, it's easier to pick up new habits if we stack them onto old habits. By linking your new habits to a cycle that is already built into your brain, you make it more likely that you'll stick to the new behavior.

For example, many of us already have the habit of making coffee for ourselves in the morning. What if we put our journal next to the coffee maker and jotted down a few thoughts, or items of gratitude, in the morning?

You're able to rewire your brain by making habits of things without going out of your way or disrupting your usual routine. The habits get added to your day-to-day—you don't set aside a special time for them, so to speak.

The more you do something, the more synaptic pruning occurs. If you habit stack, you'll expedite the learning curve of developing any new habit and incorporating it into your life. Just think about it: if you tell yourself to say a prayer before bed every night and keep up with it, it'll become second nature.

Don't Just Play to Your Strengths; Identify and Work On Your "Keystone Weaknesses"

People always say play to your strengths, not your weakness, but that's not the best piece of advice. While it's true that we ought to play to our strengths, some weaknesses are "keystone weaknesses."

Like keystone habits, keystone weaknesses play into your life in a multitude of ways. They're super important skill sets that everyone needs to have a modicum of ability in. Otherwise, you'll have cracks in your dam and be ill-equipped when the floodwaters start pouring.

With my clients, their keystone weaknesses often tend to revolve around motivation, time, and money. They'll say something like, "I don't like staring at spreadsheets, so I'm gonna stop doing a budget and spending so much time on my finances." To me, that's just another way to say, "I want to get bitten in the butt."

If you don't want to deal with something critical because it's difficult for you, that philosophy will come back to haunt you time and time again. If you neglect finances because they stress you out, the unfortunate reality is that they'll stress you out twice as much when money problems inevitably arise.

The Currency of Investing in Yourself Is Time, Not Money

When it comes to investing in yourself, people usually assume it means allocating a budget for self-growth activities. They believe you can pay for some sage advice, start hitting the mat at the local yoga studio, fly off to Tibet for a "spiritual awakening," or hire a personal coach like me.

These are valid options to pursue, don't get me wrong. They can be positive additions to your life. But, again, all of that will be for nothing if you don't go into those investments with the right mindset.

Whether you're burned-out or suffering from an emotional storm, there's no tried-and-true solution that won't require some serious self-reflection. The right amount of money or the right app won't get your life in order if you don't do the work behind the scenes. You'll end up stuck in an endless search for the right tool or technique instead of living out your calling.

Many of my clients come to me because they're trying to earn more time and money and think nothing is wrong with their mentality. The success brought on by their talents gives them an over-confident attitude, and their cockiness creates more problems for them. In contrast to Peder's situation, their talent is going to their head and fostering a lack of discipline just as detrimental to their belief system as putting themselves down.

The point is, it doesn't matter how rich you are on the outside if you aren't rich on the inside. Investing in yourself lies in behavioral work: working on your mindsets, beliefs, attitude, habits, and so on. But that's harder, and that's why so many people struggle to get there. Self-growth doesn't come overnight, and people lose patience. They can't say no to things that serve as nothing but vices. For example, they struggle to learn delayed gratification—that you can have anything, but you can't have everything.

Without patience, consistency, and determination, it'll be impossible to put in the behavioral work required to invest in yourself.

Investing in Yourself Is First and Foremost

Investing in yourself is the equivalent of starting to build your puzzle by filling in the edges—it's the process that makes the rest of the puzzle a piece of cake. Only after you've invested in yourself can you invest in others, develop your influence, and impact the world.

However, many of my clients fall short the moment they approach their calling as if it's not a puzzle but is, instead, a tree with high-hanging fruit and low-hanging fruit. Investing in themselves gets treated like something they can wait till later to do, as if it's not as important as making money or freeing up their time to pursue their calling. Instead of trying to fix things from the ground up, they pursue objectives that prove unsafe for their stress levels and sleeping habits.

From there, it's a domino effect. Their day job suffers, their calling gets put on the back-burner, and they grow burned-out and frustrated as they bang their heads against the wall with well-known tactics that seem to only fall short for them. If they had started with investing in themselves and putting in that behavioral work, things wouldn't be unraveling—there would be a more solid foundation to work from.

No one is going to produce their best work if they don't have the passion for the work, right? And no one is going to have a passion for their work if they need to rush it, right? Every part of the equation is going to be interconnected and working in tandem. It's a loop or circle, not a line. Every component is important on the path toward your vision, and every positive thing will only ever reinforce the others—it's not so black-and-white. Before you can start investing in others, developing an influence, or impacting the world, it all starts with investing in yourself.

You don't just wake up and become a butterfly—growth is a process. It's all tied together—there's no one "simple fix." Living out your calling is a collection of puzzle pieces making up a jigsaw; it's a series of cogs that compose one well-oiled machine.

If there's a weak link, the whole chain will fall apart. For many of my clients, that weak chain is investing in themselves. It's a journey, not a race, and you'll set yourself up for failure if you don't prioritize investing in yourself.

Chapter Summary

Limiting beliefs are mental poison that will sabotage you from the micro to macro level. They lead to self-fulfilling prophecies and crushed dreams. One of the best ways to overcome limiting beliefs is to replace them with enabling truths.

Your beliefs are what will drive your behaviors and habits, which weigh on your entire picture from a macro to micro level. We must reinforce habits that align with achieving our priorities, while reforming habits that don't get us closer to living out our calling. If you want to invest in others, develop an influence, impact the world, and master your time, treasures, and talents, it all starts with you. If you want to live out your calling, you must begin by learning how to invest in yourself.

Key Takeaways

- Review your keystone strengths and weaknesses.
- Examine whether your recurring thoughts fit the 3 Ps.

- Give the habit loop hacking exercise a try.
- Write down one limiting belief you have and replace it with an enabling truth.

Chapter 2:

Invest in Others

· · · · · · · · · · · ·

Rain poured down in buckets, and I was covered in mud from head to toe. Water rockets were today's agenda for my middle school science students and, boy, it was starting to feel like a field trip to a water park.

Things were getting messy, but the hands-on learning had an awesome effect on all the kids. I found a way to make learning enjoyable for them—an objective I had been pouring my blood, sweat, and tears into achieving.

√ construction paper

√ scissors

√ tape

√ soda bottle

√ ruler

√ cork

√ inflating needle

√ cardboard

√ marker

~~change of clothes~~

Aerodynamics, hydrodynamics, and "space exploration" had never been so fun.

Suddenly, I felt a tap on my shoulder. My clothes were so wet, it sounded like somebody stepping in a puddle. I turned around to see my colleague. They came to remind me that I was late for a very important appointment. Amid all the glee and games, I completely forgot that I had been selected as a candidate for the Trinity Excellence in Teaching Award. My big interview was that day. I had no time to spare; I'd have to show up muddy and wet.

Hard Work Gets You Far

This was the culmination of years of hard work I had put in toward helping the next generation of Americans become literate in science and math. During my second year of teaching, I was "volun-told" to go to Project 2061, a long-term project centered on increasing scientific literacy. Instead of treating it like another box to check, or even a punishment, I rolled up my sleeves and worked hard. That's where I found the water rocket exercise. My work with Project 2061 was why the Trinity award panel had selected me.

I didn't think the interviewers would feel too enthused about one of their candidates showing up covered in mud, but, to my surprise, they seemed to like it. The commitment and experiential approach I was wearing came across as admirable to the panel interviewing me.

I ended up winning the award, but I definitely wouldn't recommend showing up to your next interview like that. If not for my work on Project 2061, I'm sure they'd have chosen one of the other candidates. Maybe one who had enough manners to at least wear some pressed khaki pants and a buttoned shirt. That's more like what I wore to my second interview when I was selected for the award again six years later.

Jeff Brown: Discover Your Calling to Serve Others

Jeff Brown is a coach and podcaster who loves to help other people clarify their calling and make sure their mindset serves their vision.

If there's any question in recent history that's stumped more people in our culture, it's "What's my calling in life?" Endless content has been written and recorded on the subject, promising to unlock your potential and transform your life. Unfortunately, so many of these bold promises come down to clever marketing, not real answers. The truth is that only God knows your true calling, no one else. However, there's something you can do to get closer: adopt an abundance mindset.

Before you do that, it's important to distinguish "career" from "calling." Career is what you get paid to do, whereas calling is what you're made to do. Sometimes they intersect, sometimes they're identical, and sometimes they're mutually exclusive. Whatever your case is, make that distinction first. Second, realize that adopting an abundance mindset involves doing two very uncomfortable things regularly: admitting when you're wrong and admitting when you don't know something. This is crucial for leaving your ego at the door and expanding your horizons.

Next up, understand that your calling is not all about you. In both my career and calling, the through line was about more than just me—it was about teaching and training others. To see things abundantly, I had to go outside myself, distill and put my own stamp on what I learned, and teach it to others. The more I did this, the more I loved what I did. That's the key to making your calling so much more.

Finally, if you're itching to expand your mental horizons, read. Read voraciously. I used to think that men like Steve Jobs or Bill Gates were untouchable, destined for greatness, while I wasn't. But that was never true. The truth was that books helped me develop an abundance mindset, allowing me to become someone I never thought I could be. As a result, I enjoyed my career and pursued my calling all at the same time. That's the beauty of an abundance mindset.

Investing in Others Started with Investing in Myself

> The way to an abundance mindset is, quite simply, to be a voracious reader.
> —Jeff Brown

Getting to this point in my life took time, patience, and effort. But it took deliberate effort and intentional actions more than anything. This was the culmination of the long process of working toward my calling. Remember: it's a process, not an event.

Before I had an opportunity to impact the world through Project 2061, I first had to develop an influence in the community I taught in. Before I could develop an influence, I had to understand what it meant to invest in others. And, before I could begin to invest in others, I had to invest in myself.

I've said it before, and I'll say it again: each piece of the puzzle is connected. If you want to have the big picture, you'll need to fill in all the gaps and missing pieces. I told you that investing in yourself is like filling in the edges—from there, the rest is a piece of cake. Investing in others is easy once you know how to treat yourself with love and respect.

Don't Skip Stepping Stones

You must deeply understand how to walk before you turn around to help others take their first steps. You must have something in your cup if you want to pour a drink for somebody else. Your candle must be lit to share the flame. The analogies are endless, but the point is the same: you can't invest in others without first investing in yourself.

So, let's refresh ourselves on what it means to invest in ourselves. More importantly, I want to make it clear why investing in others is impossible if you don't first invest in yourself. It's a two-way street: the more of an "Active Relationship" you have—the more you invest in others—the more you can invest in yourself.

In a nutshell, investing in yourself means recalibrating your focus and looking at the big picture. Where are you right now and where do you want to go? In other words, ask yourself the hard questions:

- What's holding you back?
- What do you want?
- What are your strengths and weaknesses?
- What habits can you implement to either reinforce or reform those strengths and weaknesses?

To gain control, we begin by "injecting" tools, techniques, and so on. In the end, we aim to change our behavior positively. Through this, we feel less like an imposter and more like our true selves. It involves outgrowing our limiting beliefs and bad habits before ingraining better ones.

From there, shortcomings and failures give you opportunities to live, learn, and grow. You'll have control of your thoughts. They will encourage you rather than bring you down. Plus, reformed habits will give you the lifestyle you need to achieve your objectives. Refreshed with a newfound sense of confidence to fervently pursue your area of passion and live out your calling, you'll be ready to serve as a guide for others.

Investing in Others Helped Me Identify My Calling

Thousands of candles can be lighted from a single candle, and the life of the candle will not be shortened. Happiness never decreases by being shared.

—Buddha

I learned early in life that when you light another candle, you lose nothing of your own—you just create more light.

I grew up as a young man in the Christian Church. I was always a smart, nerdy kid. I was always sticking my nose in some book and, while I was never one of the popular kids, I did very well in an academic sense. I had friends who I'd hang out with, but I wasn't too social.

Despite not being a social butterfly, I always enjoyed helping others. I realized I didn't just enjoy learning about stuff but also tutoring other people. Whenever there was an opportunity to speak in front of the class, I'd line up front and center. Thus, early on, I knew where to start looking for my calling. I had a hunch I was meant to operate in the area of educating, teaching, or helping others in ways that involved speaking.

Your Calling Isn't Your Career or Your Degree

> Career is what you're paid to do, calling is what you're made to do.
> —Jeff Brown

I went to college—Texas A&M University—with the idea of becoming a medical researcher, and successfully earned a degree in biochemistry and genetics. That might not seem like a route to public speaking, but I looked at the big picture.

Part of it was this idea of helping others in a big way, but it also seemed something that lent itself to some of my strengths around thinking, problem-solving processes, research, and so on. Thus, it seemed like a good degree I could wrap my head around without losing my alignment with my calling.

But, boy, was I wrong: my degree opened up some unpleasant opportunities. I found myself in a job that had nothing to do with exploring my calling. I did research work in a lab, and I didn't want to do that by any means. There was too much politics and money-grubbing in the industry I was in—the opposite of investing in others. The work also revolved around doing the things I didn't love to do.

That said, there were moments of really feeling like I was getting closer to my calling. After enjoying an opportunity to go work at a middle school and help them with the science fair, I felt the embers of enthusiasm being stoked. This opportunity at the science fair really lit a fire under me. I felt the warmth that radiates from within once you begin investing in others.

Soon enough, I pivoted. I became a schoolteacher after going through an alternative certification program. From there, the sky was the limit.

Before I Could Teach, I First Had to Be Taught

> The through line is teaching and training.
> —Jeff Brown

Let's get something straight, though: I didn't pivot into becoming a teacher overnight. I put in a ton of work behind the scenes to develop my teaching skill. In other words, I invested in myself before I began to foray into investing in others.

I put time and energy into not just learning a curriculum to regurgitate it but also how to communicate with students. I studied what it took to get along with others (students and staff alike), how to speak better, and so on. Additionally, I looked for opportunities to tutor other people, connect, and invest in others.

My first teaching gig was on the south side of San Antonio in a low socioeconomic school. I taught two periods in the cafeteria, and then I moved to two other classrooms during the day while they built some new classrooms. That would probably have been fine if I had been in charge of a low-key class, but I was hosting large bodies of students and trying to teach them about something as hard to grasp as science. It got wild. But it also felt right.

I knew I wasn't very good at it yet—the alternative certification program was a crash course at best—so I immediately began to try to learn more and invest in myself. I began to connect with other teachers and ask what they were doing. Then, I took workshops and courses on how to teach science better. In my spare time, I read books and tried things out in class, doing more and more experiential learning.

Investing in Myself + Investing in Others = Developing My Influence + Impacting the World

After putting in all the work to develop my teaching abilities and then sharing those abilities with my students, results started to appear. I was invited to a workshop. I had opportunities to volunteer to work in science reform. I joined Project 2061. I began working in all of these different areas and working on the *Benchmarks for Science Literacy*.[1]

After exploring those avenues, I moved to teach at a high school in the same area and, later, I moved to a private school in downtown San Antonio (still teaching science). In each of these classes, I continued to develop how I taught and invested in myself. I invested in my classroom and my students and looked for ways to make them better at what they were doing.

---

1   American Association for the Advancement of Science, *Benchmarks for Science Literacy*, AAAS, accessed November 28, 2023, https://www.aaas.org/resources/benchmarks-science-literacy.

Overall, I found myself developing an influence in each of those communities in those classrooms, but also in the larger education community. That all started with investing in others—and investing in others all started with investing in myself.

When You Get All Wrapped Up in Yourself, You Make a Pretty Small Package

I can't emphasize enough how you must invest in yourself before you invest in others, but it's equally important for you to understand where the emphasis lies. Investing in yourself is critical, but only you can enjoy that. Investing in others is how you bring value to the world and create ripples.

Thus, investing in yourself is intended to set you up for investing in others—it provides the foundation for the rest of the puzzle. But developing an influence and impacting the world all happens through investing in others. In other words, investing in others is how you change the world, but it's impossible to invest in others without first learning to invest in yourself.

There's a common mistake, though: Sometimes people invest too much in themselves, or invest too much in others, instead of having harmony. You can't sustainably invest in yourself more than you invest in others (and vice versa). That's like aiming a rowboat toward a dock and exerting more force with one hand than the other—you'll go off-course.

The objective of investing in yourself isn't to become the strongest person, the smartest person, or the most talented person. The intention is to work on your ship, so it's sturdy enough to allow others aboard. Your aim should be to get your own feet on solid ground before showing the path to the next person.

So, to make this principle as plain as possible, let me give you a hypothetical scenario about a game most people know—soccer. Whether you play the sport or not isn't important; I aim to convey how easily you can sabotage your hopes and dreams when you overemphasize investing in yourself and underemphasize investing in others.

Meet Ethan

Meet Ethan. His calling is playing soccer. He's the captain of his college team, but that's not enough. He wants to go pro. As a smart and capable person, he understands this can't happen if he doesn't first invest in himself. He takes this very seriously before his final season of soccer begins.

Naturally, then, he leaps into action. He gets intentional and starts putting in the hard work. First, he shuts his inner critic up by replacing his limiting beliefs with enabling truths. Next, he starts reinforcing good habits and reforming bad habits by hacking the habit loop as well as habit stacking. All in all, he implements the lessons I taught in chapter 1.

Eventually, the results start showing up. His skills improve. He gets sponsored by a local sports agent, and that agent provides Ethan with the nicest cleats, a diet program, and the best ball money can buy.

Ethan is sure his team is going to win the championship, and he's going to be the MVP. And when Ethan holds that MVP trophy, sitting pretty with colorful confetti sprinkling around him, he's sure those talent scouts from the big leagues will be drooling over him.

For the time being, however, Ethan thinks he ought to focus on himself. So, he hires a personal trainer to do daily workouts in the dawn hours. He practices rain or shine with his special ball and doesn't share it with anyone else so as not to risk losing or damaging it. He watches YouTube videos for hours on end so he can "break ankles" with top-of-the-line skill moves that would humble Lionel Messi.

Overall, Ethan sticks to his lane and homes in on the objectives that will help him to build his talents. He doesn't care about what anyone else on the team needs or wants and, more importantly, he doesn't want his teammates to get better than he is. Why help them with their workouts or let them use his fancy ball? They'll be a threat if they take the spotlight, won't they?

When the offseason ends, practice starts back up. Ethan shows up to the first practice and quickly realizes his team never got the memo about investing in themselves. While Ethan woke up at 5 a.m. every morning during the summer and hit the gym with a mission, the team's goalie slept in and hit up a fast food joint for breakfast.

Ethan certainly put in the hard hours to work toward his calling, but he did that all alone. Now the championship isn't so likely. Ethan wanted a one-man show, so he'd stand out, but this really backfired. Now, living out what he thinks to be his calling—playing professional soccer—seems more like a pipe dream than a potential reality. After all, professional scouts might not see him if his team never even makes it to the playoffs.

Meet Nick

Meet Nick. Unlike Ethan, Nick has a collaborative, abundant mindset. He's not stuck in that scarcity mentality of getting ahead of his teammates and hoarding all the glory for himself. He's a real team player with a passion for having fun with his brothers-in-shin-pads. In other words, Nick doesn't prioritize investing in himself over investing in others.

Nick still has his eyes on the prize—going pro, winning the championship, you name it—but he's not trying to climb over other players. He wants to elevate them. He's a real captain, trying to work together with his buddies. He knows a chain is only as strong as its weakest link, and he also knows how much the other players on the team care about the sport of soccer.

Instead of keeping that ball for himself, Nick holds a scrimmage with his teammates twice a week and kicks that ball around until it's unusable and deflated. He goes so far as to create personalized circuit training regimens for his teammates based on what he was taught by his personal trainer. All ships begin to rise higher, Nick acts as a true steward, and he showcases the value of investing in others. He's shifted the focus away from what he wants and instead focuses on what everyone on the team wants—a winning attitude.

It turns out that everyone wants that championship just as badly as Nick does—they just needed a kick in the butt. When they realize how well investing in yourself has worked for Nick, they start picking up what he's putting down. In other words, Nick's hard work becomes contagious.

Before Nick knows it, the team has the makings of championship victors, with an undefeated season to boot. And when the guys do win that championship, that's not what matters to Nick. What feels even better than that trophy or that professional contract he gets offered or his achievement of living out his calling is the camaraderie he helped build.

Nick can feel pride knowing of the memories he helped forge for everyone. Nick feels a true sense of purpose, without a doubt, and he can rejoice in the fact that he has helped his teammates to feel the same. He's built friendships that may last a lifetime, created a legacy with his actions, developed an influence, and impacted the world in a special way.

That's a lot more than Ethan can say, isn't it?

Making a Mark on the World Begins with Your Mentality

The power of investing in others goes far beyond team sports. If your priorities are only based on yourself and gaining more, you'll never be content. You'll never have that satisfaction that comes with fulfilling a purpose greater than yourself.

Ambition isn't wrong, but selfish ambition is. You can be content with what you have to show for yourself or excited about what you might be able to accomplish, but having self-centered intentions will set you up for failure. That failure could manifest in the form of living an emotional lie, ending up "successful" but lonely, or seeing mediocre results that leave you unsatisfied. By retaining the ambition to grow and do bigger things for the kingdom—by investing in others—you can keep working hard without losing sight of what matters most.

Stewardship is something that will serve you in every facet of your life, endowing you with a mentality that leaves smiles in your wake and success on your horizon. Investing in yourself will set you up for success in your own life, but developing your influence and impacting the world is impossible without investing in others.

By adopting the mentality of showing up for others, doing the right thing, helping other people, and paying it forward, you'll go further. It doesn't matter whether you have a big job title or not. You can be a minor or major member of a community—all that matters is looking for opportunities to help someone else and doing so. That's how you leave a legacy and make your mark on the world.

> Great achievement is usually born of great sacrifice,
> and is never the result of selfishness.
>
> **— Napoleon Hill**

Develop an Abundance Mindset

If you've ever seen the 1999 film *The Matrix*, there's a scene that has grown famous in pop culture. The protagonist, Neo, is offered the option of taking a blue pill or a red pill. These two pills essentially offer two separate paths for Neo; if Neo takes the red pill, he will learn potentially unsettling or life-changing truths. But if he takes the blue pill, Neo will remain in contented ignorance.

When it comes to investing in others, these two pills exist in different forms. The red pill offers an abundant mindset and the willingness to invest your time and energy into the betterment of others. The blue pill offers a selfish, scarcity mindset where investing in others isn't perceived to be as important as investing in yourself.

In the examples of Ethan and Nick, Ethan took the blue pill while Nick took the red pill. Those examples were centered on hypothetical scenarios in a sport you may not even care about, but the message is what I want to get across. Whether it comes to a season of soccer, your career, your family, or your friendships, the point remains: you can either contribute to a bigger picture or grow disillusioned building your puzzle all alone.

The Currency of Investing in Others Is Time—Not Money

You don't need to be a wealthy philanthropist to be loved and recognized for your altruism. Those who take the red pill feel fulfilled daily, no matter how much money they have. They know they're not only developing themselves but developing an influence and impacting the world through small acts of kindness.

Then we have greedy hoarders of their wealth, people frightened of losing things, striving to keep up with the Joneses and never giving a penny away. They, on the other hand, surely took the blue pill. They'll do anything to stay on top, whether that means making someone else take the fall, or playing dirty. These people might very well climb to the top, but they'll live life through clenched teeth and closed fists. They'll never create the same legacy or find the same fulfillment as the person who took the red pill.

Again, investing in others and having the mentality of stewardship isn't about donating the most money or being the most liked. It's about being committed to caring about others and taking measures to help others. When I won teaching awards or landed a spot in Project 2061, I wasn't the most knowledgeable science teacher out there. I didn't churn out class after class of Ivy League valedictorians. When I first became a teacher and started teaching new material to my students, I could only keep one chapter ahead of the curriculum. I was only ever able to stay one step further in prep work.

I was never the best at the subjects I taught. I wasn't a master by any means. But I made sure I was never behind so that I could still bring my kids along. Having a driving reason to help my students be the best they could be was enough to find enormous success in developing an influence and impacting the world. The willingness to help others is all you need to create long-lasting ripples that will give your life more meaning and purpose than ever before.

We're Meant to Be a River, Not a Reservoir

We're meant to be a river, not a reservoir. As things flow into us, they're meant to flow back out again. If all they do is flow in and stay there, it gets stagnant. Life grows mundane and meaningless. Happiness is hard to find in those murky waters.

If you only ever focus on investing in yourself, you're never going to be content. Human beings are relational creatures. We want to help others. However, I'd go so far as to say that those who are reading this book have explored this innate part of human

nature more than the majority of folks. The fact that you're reading this chapter shows a commitment to investing in others.

Now, make sure you understand the big picture. Invest in
yourself first, but never to the detriment of others. Use your time,
the most valuable currency out there, to leave a trail of smiles in
your wake. Share the flame in your candle. This will reveal your
personal calling like nothing else can.

Chapter Summary

Before I could begin developing an influence and impacting the
world as a teacher, I had to put in work behind the scenes to invest
in myself so that I could invest in others. Likewise, investing in
yourself is necessary to invest in others, but it shouldn't be the
only thing you do. If your priorities are only based on yourself and
gaining more, you'll never be satisfied.

There are two "pills" when it comes to investing in others:
the "blue pill" and the "red pill." The red pill offers an abundant
mindset and the willingness to invest your time and energy into
the betterment of others. The blue pill offers a selfish, scarcity
mindset where investing in others isn't perceived to be as important as investing in yourself.

Key Takeaways

- Examine how you can invest in other people, wherever
  you find yourself in life and career.
- Take a long, hard look at how you spend your time. Does
  it all go back into yourself? Or, do you intentionally block
  out time to invest in other people?
- As you invest in others, take note of what makes you feel
  passionate. This will begin to reveal your personal calling.

Chapter 3:

Develop Your Influence

. . . .

Once upon a time, there lived an old man who used to go to the ocean to do his writing. He had a habit of walking on the beach every morning before he began his work. The salty air and serene environment inspired him in his artistic pursuits.

Early one morning, he was walking along the shore after a big storm had passed and found the vast beach littered with starfish as far as the eye could see, stretching in both directions. Off in the distance, the old man noticed a small boy approaching.

As the boy walked, he paused every so often and bent down. As he grew closer, the man could see that he was bending down to pick up an object and throw it into the sea. The boy came closer still and the man called out, "Good morning! May I ask what it is that you are doing?"

The young boy paused, looked up, and replied, "Throwing starfish into the ocean. The tide has washed them up onto the beach, and they can't return to the sea by themselves. When the sun gets high, they will die, unless I throw them back into the water."

The old man replied, "But there must be tens of thousands of starfish on this beach. I'm afraid you won't be able to make much of a difference."

The boy bent down, picked up yet another starfish, and threw it as far as he could into the ocean. Then he turned, smiled, and said, "It made a difference to that one!"

Aaron Walker: Growth, Opportunity, and Influence

Businessman and Life Coach, Aaron T. Walker, has inspired many through his leadership, mentorship, and consistent pursuit of excellence. He enjoys helping others and believes experience is a great teacher. 35 years of entrepreneurship and marriage have given Aaron a wealth of experience.

As we grow in our careers, the Lord blesses many of us with new opportunities to influence others in our journeys. He may place us in charge of a congregation, help us steward the success of a company, or allow us to help a select few folks improve themselves. It's a blessing to influence others. However, it's also a massive responsibility, and so many folks misuse that opportunity. If the Lord has allowed you to be a leader to others, here are some best practices to remember.

First, your influence can easily become manipulation if you're not careful. I once told a prospect that another person was interested in the same property he was, but in truth, that "another person" had already declined the offer. So, what I told the prospect was manipulative—I wanted him to close the deal faster out of a false sense of urgency. This may seem harmless, but as a leader stewarding God's people, you have to be ultra-careful to not steer people in the wrong direction. We have the highest standard to follow.

Next, you have to realize that money won't scratch the itch like you want it to. Sure, money is important to any business and can be used to help others, but if that's what you prioritize as a leader, you'll find yourself always wanting more out of yourself and those you lead. Instead, figure out what fulfills you and plays to the strengths God gave you. In the four decades I've been doing this, that approach always brings the most out of me and my people.

Finally, to be a good leader, focus on adding value to your people, not just "being a good leader." By concentrating on adding value, you'll naturally develop as a leader and help develop those under you. Most importantly, thank the Lord for this opportunity and watch over your sheep just like Jesus watches over you.

Everyone Can Throw a Starfish

When someone speaks of developing an influence, people typically misinterpret that as becoming an influential celebrity. They create a limiting belief right off the bat and set themselves up for disappointment with entirely unrealistic objectives.

They might not believe they need to become the next Elon Musk or Bill Gates, but they still see the word "influence" as synonymous with "famous person." The fact is, everyone can make an impact on the world whether they work in an isolated cubicle, cover night shifts at the local diner, or do part-time teaching at a kindergarten. It's a matter of perspective.

I'm here to help you impact the world based on whatever the world means to you. The ripples we put into the world are often much larger than we know, and it's up to us to put positive ripples out.

> When I was a young man, I wanted to change the world.
> I found it was difficult to change the world, so I tried to change my nation.
> When I found I couldn't change the nation, I began to focus on my town.
> I couldn't change the town and as an older man, I tried to change my family.
> Now, as an old man, I realize the only thing I can change is myself, and suddenly I realize that if long ago I had changed myself, I could have made an impact on my family.
> My family and I could have made an impact on our town.
> Their impact could have changed the nation and I could indeed have changed the world.
> **—Author Unknown**

In other words, you don't need to be on the front page of the paper to develop influence. You can impact the world by impacting just one person. Developing your influence doesn't mean changing the whole world or altering the lives of everybody on the planet. It means impacting the world in terms of the world that you live in—the people in your community, the people in your inner circle, your clients, your family, your friends, your church, and so on.

Investing in Others Is about Learning Compassion; Developing Your Influence Is about Learning Leadership Skills

> What's important to you is what you actually do, not what you say.
> —Aaron Walker

First of all, know that you influence everyone around you, all the time. Have you ever worked in a place where one coworker came in and had a really sour mood? What tends to happen, in that instance, is they begin to drag others down with them. People begin walking on eggshells, or even start being short and snappy with others in their interactions. On the other hand, if a coworker comes in feeling chipper and excited to start the day, it tends to lift the spirits of everyone around them, if only by a little bit.

In other words, these two coworkers are leading other people to feel a certain way. Leadership is synonymous with influence. Influence is leadership, and leadership is influence. If you want to influence other people positively, you must learn how to lead.

In the last chapter, we talked about investing in others. I spoke of how stewardship is a mentality that will take you far in life. When the focus is shifted from decorating your yacht to getting all ships in the cove to rise higher, you'll end up with a fleet rather than a showboat. Simply put, compassion makes the difference when it comes to investing in yourself and others.

Taking action to help others grow, succeed, benefit, and more will help us greatly in life. We can't take those steps without investing in ourselves, however, meaning we must be walking the walk before we help another person take their first steps.

And while investing in others will teach you the life skills of compassion and teamwork as well as the asset of an abundance mindset, developing your influence is how you get people to take action on their behalf. Because at the end of the day, people will only accept as much help as they want to accept. You can bend over backward to invest in them but, if you don't develop an influence, your efforts will be in vain.

So, if you want to influence people through your effort, you must go beyond compassion into leadership. Feeling compassion for someone is extremely helpful, don't get me wrong. However, how many people see a sad commercial on television asking for donations to a charity, feel compassion for a moment, and then forget about it seconds later when a pizza commercial comes on? Compassion requires action if it is to turn into a positive influence. The better an individual becomes at leading themselves and others, the more the influence is amplified.

Wait, Am I Just Manipulating People?

> It can become manipulation when your motivation isn't correct.
> **—Aaron Walker**

As you invest in others with compassion and action, you naturally begin influencing them. However, don't put the cart before the horse: You must invest in other people before you can influence them positively. If you try to influence people without investing in them, they will either ignore your influence, or worse, you'll influence them negatively. Remember, leadership is influence, and influence is leadership.

Once you've mastered the art of investing in others, you're ready to begin leading people and developing your influence. If you've been reading between the lines, you might have already thought about an important question: What is the difference between influencing and manipulating? After all, we've all been in situations where it felt like people were just trying to manipulate us for their own purposes, even if they claimed to have the best intentions. Now, as we set about on our journey to impact the world through our calling, we don't want to make the same mistake.

Here's my best definition of manipulation versus influence:

- **Manipulation**: Getting somebody else to do something because it's in your best interests. Self-centered.

Here's an example: Say you want to hire an employee to work at your restaurant. You want them to learn how to cook, clean the dishes, and bus the tables. You teach them the bare minimum, treating them as another cog in the machine. You don't take the time to get to know them or understand their goals. All you care about is making more money for your restaurant business. This is manipulation, treating people as pawns to serve your own interests (even if your restaurant is a good cause in your mind!).

- **Influencing**: Getting somebody else to do something because it's in their best interests. Centered on others.

Now, take the example of owning a restaurant again. In this case, you find an employee who is passionate about the restaurant industry and wants to open their own place one day. You teach them the skills they need for the job and invest in the growth of their own business acumen. Instead of thinking about your own interests, you focus on how this job will benefit the employee you hired.

Going beyond that, the influencer opens a restaurant to put smiles on their patron's faces and promote the art and craft of cooking. The manipulator opens it to make money and treats customers as walking wallets.

To sum it up, intent matters. Now, you might ask, if the influencer hires an employee and seeks that employee's best interests, doesn't it secretly and indirectly serve the owner's best interests anyway? Yes. Frankly, it's impossible to avoid self-interest on some level. So, what we do is synchronize the interests of others with our own interests, and still put their interests first. If you can do that, you can win in any area of life.

One business owner put it like this: "My entire job is to help other people get what they want. That's all I focus on. Why? Because I know that if I spend all my time helping other people get what they want, then what I want will come as a natural consequence."

> You can have everything in life you want if you will just
> help enough other people get what they want.
> —Zig Ziglar

The fact that you're wondering about manipulation and influence means you have a good heart. If you've never thought about avoiding manipulation, then I would be concerned. In fact, a general rule of thumb is that if you're *asking yourself whether you're being manipulative*, you're probably not being manipulative. It's usually those who don't ask themselves those questions who end up having the biggest problems.

Everyone will make an impact on both themselves and others—it's up to us to decide what sort of impact we want to make. Sometimes we want to make a good impact, but we simply aren't investing in others as much as we believe. It's hard to define the line because sometimes you may be convinced you're acting in the best interests of somebody else only to realize you're not serving them. Still, you can train yourself to think in terms of how others will benefit instead of how you will benefit.

Think of a sleazy used car salesman. They want to make a sale, no matter what. To this end, they may bend the truth, or try to lock customers into a bad financial situation. This salesman thinks in terms of self-interest. Now think of a great and good salesman. Instead of trying to make a sale, they simply focus on creating happy customers. They know that if they work for the real benefit of whoever comes to the lot, then sales will come as a natural consequence. There's a reason the best marketers focus on making a difference to just one customer rather than playing dirty to make better dividends.

I actually worked as a car salesman for a year or so. I saw so many sales that put the buyer in a bad situation. I remember an eighteen-year-old who came in, and one of my colleagues convinced him to roll out of the dealership in a retro sports car, for zero down and a monthly payment of $800. His income was less than $2,000 a month. It was awful. On the other hand, I also saw salesmen who would actually tell a potential customer no if the purchase wasn't in their best interest. Guess which salesmen had people come in and ask for them by name when they were ready to purchase?

> Leadership is influence, nothing more, nothing less.
> —John C. Maxwell

Developing an Influence Narrows Your Calling Down

As you read this book, you'll realize more and more that discovering your calling isn't some light switch. Some of us never know whether we've found our calling, despite how much we end up developing an influence and impacting the world.

Take me, for example. Right now, coaching is the most authentic fit for me. But that might change; I may find something else. I want to do other things and test those out and see whether something else feels more like it's authentically what I'm called to do. As I coach my clients to do, it's worth testing the waters and getting feedback. Only through experimentation can we see whether there's a pivot we ought to make to be closer to our true calling.

When I became a school teacher, I was experimenting. I had to read the books, study, and spend time and energy building toward my current self. I didn't know I liked public speaking until I had done it. It took investing in myself and investing in others to gain influence, and things became more clear once I had that influence. I saw that I was able to make an impact through my current pursuits, a telltale sign that I was doing something right when it came to finding what my calling might be.

None of us know what our calling is on day one. Some of us never find out and take our last breath without ever figuring out what we were put on the earth for. But having a vague concept of what you're interested in is enough to start; from there you can experiment and move closer and closer to finding where your heart is.

Finding your calling is iterative, and dialing into it is a multifaceted process that doesn't happen overnight. The more you explore your calling, the more feedback you'll get. That feedback can either serve as a fuel that tells you that you're on the right trajectory, or it will let you know you're on the wrong path.

In fact, getting frustrated with the feedback is a positive part of the process. People tend to think some emotions are bad, particularly when they're negative, but they're not bad emotions if we don't let them get under our skin and elicit a dramatic response from us.

If you ask me, it's better than "comfortable misery" where you grow complacent and live a life that's "comfortable" but isn't getting much of a rise out of you.

One reason a calling is so hard to nail down is that it manifests itself differently in each arena of life. Take family skills versus corporate skills. You shouldn't treat your family like they're your employees, and you shouldn't treat your employees like they're your own children. Yet, many people are called both to be a parent and be a manager, not just one of the two. The good news is that as your influence develops, you naturally find yourself getting closer to your true calling.

Developing an Influence and Living Out Your Calling Work in Tandem

> To be a good leader, concentrate on adding value, not just being a leader. You'll naturally become a leader as a result.
> —Aaron Walker

Look at areas you're already developing an influence in. And if you're struggling to develop an influence *anywhere*, then it might be a good indication that you haven't truly found your calling. From there, you can pivot and discern whether it's worth putting all that time and energy into something—is this a good fit for me?

But be sure to commit past the experimenting phase; you can't just try something for a few days and call it quits. It's a process, not an event, and progress is better than perfect. Grammarians might say, "Don't you mean progress is better than perfection?" But I kind of like saying it in a way that is intentionally imperfect. To move in a direction is okay; you don't have to fully arrive. Finding your calling doesn't mean everything will be perfect from then on out, but things should certainly be better. Discomfort can be good or bad; it can be you growing out of your comfort zone, or it can simply signify a bad match.

On the other hand, if you feel as though you are living out your calling, it will naturally develop your influence further. This happens because you're acting in a way that's congruent and authentic, and people are attracted to that. Likewise, if you're trying to develop an influence by living out a calling that isn't your true calling, people will push back on that, and you'll feel drained rather than built up. In that case, you'll need to make the pivots necessary to feed your heart and soul and live out your calling.

A Quick Caveat

It's important to remember that your calling and your career are not the same. I hinted at this a minute ago when I talked about how being a parent is a calling in itself. However, it goes beyond that. Some people find that their job has nothing to do with their calling; it just pays the bills and gives them the freedom to pursue what's really on their heart. If you can get paid to live out your calling, that's great. But your calling might be an unpaid hobby or interest you pursue on the side that has nothing to do with your nine-to-five. Does this mean you shouldn't find a job that aligns with your calling? Of course not! However, make peace with the fact that a calling is more complex than just one arena of your life.

Now, Back to the Relationship between Calling and Influence

As you begin developing your influence, it will clarify your values. You'll see things that feel important to you, and other things that really don't. You'll find yourself investing energy into certain areas to gain influence. For example, you might not have much interest in the routine tasks at your job, but you might find yourself joining a certain committee that meets after hours because it seems important to you.

All these actions will give you feedback. Again, when you operate in line with your calling, it attracts people. When you live a lie, it repulses people. You'll also gain feedback through energy. Areas that give you positive emotional energy are probably aligned with your calling. Areas that drain you, probably aren't. This doesn't mean you should only do tasks that build your energy, though: every career, hobby, passion project, and relationship will have tasks and events that drain you, even if you feel passionate about them in general.

Over time, though, you and others will recognize that you have a gift in a certain area. Or, you'll discover (and be told) that maybe you're not cut out for something. The results you get will act as a barometer for your calling. The influence you have over people will act like the temperature gauge. Observe the areas you get results, and the areas you find yourself gaining influence, and you're on the right track.

Where Do You Start?

Developing an influence—like every other piece of the puzzle—won't happen overnight. Look for incremental improvement rather than enormous leaps. It's a process, not an event. We're taking stepping stones over the river; we're not launching over it via catapult. There's no perfect formula for it, but there are fantastic waypoints along the path. Here they are:

1. Learn to Communicate

Learning to communicate could mean public speaking, yes, but it doesn't necessarily have to be oratory. Communication comes through everyday conversations, writing, and even body language. Can you take the ideas you have, crystallize them, and expand upon them? Can you make them practical for others?

This could look like starting a podcast or writing a book. Those are lofty goals, though. It might begin with simply learning how to get along better at work; learning how to get your point across to your boss and colleagues. You also need to learn how to support and raise your children through communication, and have a healthy relationship with your significant other through, you guessed it, communication.

I put it like this: Communication is what you say, and how you say it. It's also what you do, and how you do it. Your actions communicate, sometimes louder than words. So, study the art and science of clear and effective communication. If you learn how to communicate, you will be much better at influencing people.

Personally, I took the podcast route at the start. I enjoy talking, but I don't enjoy writing so much. I actually got certified in DISC as a "Human Behavior Consultant" with Personality Insights, Inc. I wanted to understand myself and others better, so I could communicate better. This and the podcast helped me develop communication skills that directly translated into the writing of this book. Learning to communicate in one area boosts your skills indirectly in the others. All are important.

2. Examine Your Roles

Most of us have a plethora of roles we serve in. Sometimes, when I coach someone, I give them five minutes to write down as many roles as they can think of. They will often come back to me with upward of forty roles! Here are a few examples: father, husband, employee, boss, hobbyist, athlete, cousin, nephew, grandson, church member, customer, salesperson, son, colleague, brother, citizen, community member, club member, entrepreneur, owner . . . the list goes on.

In every single one of these roles, you have influence. It comes in different levels, in a variety of ways—but it's there. Given that you have limited resources, where do you want to develop influence the most? You only have a finite amount of time and energy, so you need to create an aim when it comes to developing your influence. There are so many avenues to explore, and you've surely laid down the cobblestones on more than a few of them—start from there. Just don't lose sight of what's the most important thing to you vs. what'll make for the easiest path to developing an influence—what do you value the most?

3. Experiment and Learn by Doing

Pick something and go for it. Start walking forward instead of standing still and looking around. The way I like to put it is this: Look for the fire, and look for the feedback. You'll never learn what you're passionate about if you stay still. If you never put yourself out there, nobody will tell you that you have a gift (or that you're not so good at something).

Additionally, you need to commit to your experiments for at least 90 days, preferably over 150. The first three weeks of any venture is barely enough time to know anything. Keep going in the area you want to develop influence until you get genuine feedback. Be unafraid; action is inherently risky, but you have nothing to lose by trying. You have everything to lose by refusing to act and watching your life pass by.

4. Make Progress, Not Perfection

As cliché as it sounds, it's all about the journey. Consider the direction you're moving in. You may never fully arrive, so don't expect perfect results. The rubber meets the road here when we encounter negative feedback.

Just because you get negative feedback doesn't mean you're heading in the wrong direction. Criticism and difficulty may indicate that you need to push forward and suck it up in the short term. However, it could also mean that you need to pivot. How do you distinguish between stretching and misalignment?

It takes repetition and hard-earned wisdom (and you often get wisdom only through having a lack of it, and thus making a mistake). For example, the first time you speak in public, I guarantee it won't feel comfortable. But that doesn't mean you're not cut out for public speaking. Lean into it for a time, and tally up your results over ten trials instead of one. So, if the first trial is abysmal, keep going. If the tenth trial is still abysmal, you may need to form an exit strategy.

5. Influence Up

You might think, "I'm not the boss, or a parent, or a coach, or anything like that. I can't develop an influence!" That's incorrect. Regardless of where you are in the positional chain of command, you can always influence. There's a difference between positional authority and positive influence.

If you're one employee among thousands, good. What are you doing to not only make your job easier but also to make the lives of your colleagues and boss better? What are you doing to not only perform the job but to excel at it? The average American spends 40 percent of their workday *not doing work tasks*.[2] You have to choose to be different. And if you are giving 100 percent, then hey, you're already outperforming the next person by nearly double!

Everyone wants to write a book, and few do. Everyone wants to start a podcast, and few do. Almost everyone I've met wants to earn six or seven figures a year doing something they love that also gives them time for their family, their friends, and their hobbies. Almost nobody gets there. You have to make the decision to change, to be different, to develop an influence regardless of your starting position.

Be Faithful in the Little

> Passion leaves you pretty quick. The money doesn't scratch the itch like you want it to. We need a higher level of purpose and meaning.
> —Aaron Walker

Lastly, no, you don't need to earn a million dollars every year in order to have an influence or calling. Remember, you don't need to become a famous celebrity. You only need to walk forward with compassion and leadership and pay close attention to the feedback. Follow the fire, and follow the voices that give you constructive feedback.

My son has this friend. They both work at the same grocery store. In the eyes of the world, this might not be a place where one has a ton of influence. But in terms of "inspired living," this is an

---

2　Bourree Lam, "The Wasted Workday," *The Atlantic*, December 4, 2014, https://www.theatlantic.com/business/archive/2014/12/the-wasted-workday/383380/.

excellent place to be, providing an essential service to thousands of people every day, and learning so much about business and hard work. Plus, it's a fantastic proving ground.

My son's friend usually gets up late. He has thirty minutes to haphazardly follow a morning routine (if even), rush to the store, and clock in barely on time. When he clocks in, he isn't mentally prepared for the job, so he carries stress into everything he does. This gives him a negative attitude about both the work and the boss.

My son gets up at least an hour early. He shaves and showers, and he has enough time to get into the right headspace for work. Since he has time, he arrives early, takes a moment to breathe, and then shows up ready to rock when the shift starts. He finds the work easier, and his mind is open to learning new things.

Who do you think will have more positive influence at work? Who do you think the manager will choose when a spot opens for a supervising position? You and I have the same choice, every single day. We should communicate with our words and actions. We ought to play every role life has given us with honor. As we go, we'll experiment and learn with a progress-over-perfection mindset. Over time, we'll find our influence expanding. We'll be making a real impact!

Chapter Summary

Developing your influence isn't necessarily about becoming an influencer. You don't need to reach celebrity status to make an impact on the world. Developing an influence is about impacting the world based on the feedback you get regarding your calling. The ripples we put into the world are often much larger than we know. Learn to lead yourself and lead others through compassionate investment and intentional action, and you'll find your calling clarified and influence growing.

Key Takeaways

- Learn the art of communication, whether verbal, written, or even body language.
- Write down all the roles you play, and consider which to prioritize.
- Commit to experimentation and learning. Follow the fire and feedback.

Chapter 4:

Impact the World

· · · · · · · · · · · · ·

I f you've followed the world of leadership for any length of time, you've probably heard of John C. Maxwell. He's a speaker, leader, and author specializing in leadership, with a plethora of best-selling books under his belt. Surely, this is a person who has impacted the world. He's certainly impacted me with how I think about leading.

That's definitely one kind of impact. However, don't think that you need to become a larger-than-life figure in order to have an impact. In fact, some of the most impactful people don't have their name up in lights, or photos on the cover of a magazine. I can prove it to you. Without googling it, tell me the name of John C. Maxwell's father.

It's Melvin, by the way. Pat yourself on the back if you knew that one. While most people have heard of John C. Maxwell or one of his books, almost nobody remembers Melvin. This was a man who left his job at Ford to become a small-town pastor. John recalls that his dad was diligent as a pastor. He greeted everyone by name, and he knew everybody in town. By the end of his career, he had become the overseer of hundreds of churches and the president of a Christian university, which are notable achievements, but not celebrity status.

Still, nobody can doubt that Melvin Maxwell lived out his calling in multiple areas. First, he was a faithful pastor who took care of his flock, even though it didn't lead to millions of dollars or a best-selling book. Second, he raised Larry and John, together exceptionally successful in the domains of business, entrepreneurship, and ministry.

I had the privilege and pleasure of meeting Melvin myself. He shared at a John C. Maxwell event in 2015 or 2016. The accomplishments of his children were the pride of his life.

> Success is . . . knowing your purpose in life, growing to reach your maximum potential, and sowing seeds that benefit others.
> —John C. Maxwell

Today, almost nobody knows his name. And I think he'd be okay with that. Through John's and Larry's books, businesses, and ministries, his impact is still being felt all over the world.

This story inspires me for my own calling. I'm sure you've gathered from the title and chapters of this book that I want to help Christian men master their time, talent, and treasure to live out their own calling. To me, it doesn't matter whether I am a larger-than-life figure like John or something more low-key like Melvin. What matters is how I impact the people I want to influence, and how that impact ripples throughout generations.

Chris Rollins: One Simple Step at a Time

Chris Rollins is the president of Rollins Performance Group, through which he ignites, inspires, and empowers others to release the excellence that exists within them.

Success and influence don't have to be complicated, but with so many opinions flying around, how do you keep it simple? Today, I want to touch on a few foundational principles that will dispel the myths and show you what success actually looks like.

First and foremost, you have to build your foundation. Think of this like a house: Before you get to add your wall-mounted TV and chandelier, you need to build a solid foundation first. Then, you can build on top of it—first the foundation, then the walls, then the roof, and so on. However, if you never complete the first step, you can never build the rest. Start with the foundation and build from there.

Second, here's something all those gurus don't want you to hear: They're selling you cookie-cutter solutions that probably won't work for your situation. Let's say you and I agree to meet at Starbucks. Your GPS directions will be vastly different from mine. Why? Because we're coming from different starting points! The same applies to success, which is why you can't use someone else's directions.

Third, everybody loves the half-court three-pointers and dramatic leaps of faith toward success. But in reality, success almost never comes from special action—it comes from consistent action. In basketball, the classic layup scores the most points. In business, success is forged by showing up every day and doing the same, sometimes boring, actions. Today's excellence is tomorrow's average.

Finally, remember that you can't pour from an empty pitcher. A waiter can't refill your water glass if he hasn't refilled his pitcher first. So when you're out there serving others, remember that you must refill yourself first. That's how you create and build on success.

It Isn't an Overnight Discovery

I sound smart when I overcomplicate things, but don't overcomplicate things. Keep it simple.

—Chris Rollins

Our impact unravels through our lifetime. Melvin Maxwell went from making automobiles to pastoring a rural church to overseeing a church network to leading a university. All the while, he had the roles of husband and father to serve in. In each season of his life, his impact looked different.

I have had seasons of my life teaching science, serving an educational nonprofit, and working as a coach . . . and about half a dozen other things over the years. In each of them, my impact looked different, and my calling revealed itself to me more and more. No step on this journey was a waste of time or energy. Regardless of your season, you are making an outward ripple effect.

That's the difference between influence and impact. A keen reader might wonder why there's a chapter devoted to developing our influence and a whole other chapter on impacting the world. Aren't they pretty much the same thing? Not exactly.

The way I see it, your influence is over the people whose names you know. This comes in the form of your colleagues, boss, employees, students, close relationships, you name it. You don't have a tremendous amount of *influence* on people whom you simply don't know.

However, your impact is the outward ripple effect of your influence. It is more indirect and often takes more time to come to fruition. Let me give you an example: I was a science teacher for a while. Some of my students really benefited from my class, and they went on to become doctors. Perhaps some were even inspired to pursue this career through my influence. The people they help as doctors? That's part of the impact I have on the world.

It goes another step too. The students who have become doctors now have an impact of their own. Every time they help heal someone, or even save a life, they have a positive influence. Now, say they save someone's life, they go on to create a groundbreaking invention, or they become an important leader. That's part of their impact—but it may have never happened if I hadn't brought passion and dedication as a science teacher all those years ago. Do you see the outward, rippling effect?

You Have No Idea

> I can't pour into your glass from an empty pitcher.
> I have to be willing to refill my pitcher before I pour into you.
> **—Chris Rollins**

I've heard stories of people contemplating suicide, wondering whether they should go through with a plan they've made to end their own life. On the way to the cliff, they've thought, "If just one person smiles at me, I won't go through with it." Now, nobody they met woke up that day thinking, "I could make the difference between life and death with just a smile to a stranger," but they really could.

In the same way, you can impact the world greatly by simply living out your calling every day. The spirit you conduct yourself with each day will help everyone rise higher. It could be as simple as holding the door for someone or buying the coffee of the next person in line. That has a ripple effect. The difficult part is that it's tough to see. Rarely will anyone walk up to you and say, "I was planning to step off the bridge, but then you smiled at me," or "I didn't know whether I was cut out for this job, but you showed me a couple of things on the first day and gave me confidence." Still, the effect is real.

You have to stay on the ball, though. Say you're running late for work. You get caught in traffic, or you sleep through your alarm. You rush in to work, so you slip on the floor and a bunch of papers go flying out of your briefcase. You have to cram them in there and keep going. Say someone sees what's going on, opens the door for you, and asks how they can help you. That will probably make you feel much better. You'll probably begin to diffuse some of the stress you feel and show up differently to your meetings.

The problem is, we tend to focus on ourselves. We don't always see what's going on around us, what other people might need. We also don't see the connection between these small actions, the smile, the door being opened, and the impact we have on the world. If nobody thinks of you in that hurried moment, then you have a bad day in the making. Make sure that you consider your impact at the smallest level, in the daily grind, as well as the larger-than-life picture.

Influence and Impact Relate to Each Other

I've shared the difference between influence and impact, but how are they related? Do they affect one another? Yes! I'd go so far as to say that developing your influence is *how* you'll have an impact on the world. You can have a positive impact by developing the right influence.

Take those science students from back in the day. If I had a negative influence on them, it may have turned them away from a career as a doctor. In fact, I probably did have bad days that made some of my students think twice about becoming a doctor, or a teacher, or pursuing science-related studies in the future.

And that's okay. You and I will both have bad days. We'll get in a fight with our spouse in the morning. We'll get cut off in traffic and miss our exit. We'll come in late to work and fight to catch up. However, with a heart to live out our calling and a mindset to develop our influence, those days will be the exception.

We'll trend upward, toward authentic positive influence. Over time, this leads directly to a better impact on ourselves and the world around us. In fact . . .

Impacting the World Is Why I Wrote This Book

Remember how I said I don't enjoy writing very much? Yet here I am, completing a book. My "why" for completing this book is simple: I want to influence the world. John C. Maxwell was convinced to write because one of his mentors told him it would help him get his ideas out to more people. I thought that was pretty good advice. Because my calling is to help men live out their own calling through Inspired Living, I want to get the message out to as many people as possible.

Now, you're reading it. I have no idea who you are, or what year it is. I could be long gone by now, but you could be stumbling upon this. I'm having an impact that I can't even see through this. In the same way, when you live out your calling, you will have an impact beyond what you could ever know.

Impacting the World Comes One Step at a Time

> Today's excellence is tomorrow's average.
> —Chris Rollins

If there's anything I want you to take away from this chapter, it's this. Impacting the world doesn't come through huge, championship moments. It comes through showing up every day to practice with a good attitude, ready to push yourself one step forward. If you're a teacher, it comes one class at a time. If you're in the service sector, it comes one customer at a time.

Plus, it's not what you do, but the spirit behind it. Remember when we talked about the difference between influence and manipulation in the last chapter? It all comes down to your intentions. If you want to benefit yourself only, you'll manipulate others. If you actually care about the best interests of other people, you'll influence them positively.

The same goes for your impact. Walk into every arena of your life with the intent to benefit others in some small way. Add value to each environment you find yourself in. It isn't about big, flashy moments, but day-in-day-out investment.

It's Both Passive and Active

Speaking of investment, impact has both a passive and active return. In terms of impact, active returns come far less frequently. Again, few people will stop to share the impact you've had on their lives. They might not even recognize your impact or remember your name. When those few moments of recognition come, enjoy them. But don't live for them.

Instead, think of impact as the passive return of your influence. Like investing in a house, the value slowly trickles up over time if you keep paying your dues and taking care of the place. Doing everything I mentioned in the chapter about influence gives you a passive return in the form of positive impact. It's the return on your investment.

It's a Road with Many Lanes

Lastly, your impact doesn't have to look like someone else's. The world needs both Melvin Maxwell and John C. Maxwell. It needs teachers, coaches, pastors, baristas, custodians, and contractors. We need larger-than-life figures to inspire us and remind us about what could be, but we also need someone to fix our sink when it starts overflowing.

So, never diminish your own impact, or discredit the way you're changing the world. Your contribution doesn't need to look like a world-shattering revolution; it could look like raising awesome children and performing your job to the best of your ability.

How Do You Steward Your Impact?

Like everything else, growing your impact is an incremental process. You can't expect fast results. You might not even see the impact you make during your lifetime. However, we can focus on the way we influence people day in and day out and bring the intention of benefiting the world through what we do. Here are a few tactics and mindset tweaks necessary for honing your impact:

1. Make the World a Little Better than Yesterday

Performance experts will tell you that you can't get twice as good at something within a matter of weeks—but that's okay. All you need to do is get 1 percent better each day. Because I like math, let me tease this out a bit. If your skill level at, say, your job can be represented by the number 1, and you get 1 percent better, your skill level will be 1.01. That doesn't seem like a lot; in fact, it isn't. The magic comes as the investment compounds.

After fifteen days of getting 1 percent better each day, you'll actually be 16 percent better, because you get to use your current level of skill each day to invest into the next day, just like compound interest at a bank. After thirty days, you're 35 percent better. After sixty days, 82 percent. After ninety days, it's 245 percent better. Do you see the exponential increase? If you actually got 1 percent better at something every single day for three months, you'd be about 2.5 times better at it by the end of that stretch of time.

If you're a football team, and you want to win the Super Bowl, you don't need to make drastic gains every day. All you need is to get 1 percent better as a team each practice with intentionality, and you'll be ten times better by the end of the season. The same goes for the simple smile you give to people as you pass by them on the way into work, or walking over a bridge. You don't know how that investment will grow over the next few months.

2. Remove Excuses

An old TV show I love is called *M*A*S*H*, which follows a team working in a field hospital in the Korean War. It's a sitcom with some pretty serious tones. One character in the show, named Maxwell Klinger, cracks me up. He's always trying to escape the military, using a different excuse each time. He would try to run away, prove he was crazy by wearing outlandish outfits, forge fake letters, and claim different family emergencies. Ironically, he falls in love with a Korean woman and ends up staying in Korea to help her find her family after everyone else has gone home.

We can't have the Maxwell Klinger mindset if we want to have an impact. Even though he's a sitcom character, there's a little bit of him in all of us. We want to get out of our responsibilities, avoid risk, and make any excuse we can to take the easy path. We have to learn how to remove excuses from our vocabulary and mindsets, so we can show up to each arena of our lives ready to make that 1 percent investment.

3. Start Small

You can have an impact on people by cleaning the street or waiting tables. For example, one of my good friends was a bartender, even though he didn't want that job forever. Still, he showed up on time, ready to go. He worked hard to get people the food and drinks they wanted. He'll never know the impact he had in that role, but I can tell you that this attitude of service has helped him succeed in the business world like none other.

If your calling doesn't scale up like that, don't worry either. Your calling isn't a failure if you don't have ten thousand people you can point to at the end to say, "I impacted them!" Even if you can only point at one or two people you impacted, the ripples will extend further than you can realize.

As I said, if I inspired any of my students to become doctors, they might save the lives of ten thousand patients. Even though I directly influenced only one or two people, the ripples will be felt over decades and decades. Don't discount what you're doing because it's on a smaller scale than someone else.

4. Get Specific

I often ask people what they want to do with their lives. The answers vary, but much of it boils down to "I want to help people." Some people even give me that answer, word for word. That's a fantastic aspiration, but it is also vague and indefinite. Help people how? Help them with what? What will it look like? How will you know you have succeeded?

It's okay to start with a broad goal and get more specific as you go along, by the way. Just let the feedback you get help you go deeper into the areas of your passion, the areas that line up with your calling. Don't stay vague indefinitely.

This happened in my career. The common thread between teaching, working at an educational nonprofit, leading a company, and coaching? I want to help people grow and become the next level of themselves. I found that out through trial and error. I realized that teaching got me some of the way there, but I found I had better feedback when I worked with adult men on a one-on-one basis, instead of middle schoolers on a group basis.

Still, you have to start broad and get going first. Who's the first starfish you want to throw back into the ocean?

5. Improve Yourself in the Same Way You Want to Improve the World

This goes back to working on yourself first. There's a reason I put the chapter "Invest in Yourself" in this book before the chapter "Invest in Others." You want to be able to give away the absolute best version of yourself. You can't impact the world very well if you struggle in the same areas you want to help in. For example, it would be awfully weird if you wanted to become a financial advisor, but you had a ton of debt and no solid investments.

So, improve yourself the same way you want to improve the world. If you want to become a fitness coach, begin losing weight and building muscle. Work hard and be consistent. Eventually, the way you improve yourself will actually give you opportunities to improve the world in the same way. Let me show you what I mean:

If you lose twenty pounds in a matter of months, people will notice. Some of them will compliment you about it. However, a few of them will ask, "How did you do it?" That right there is an opportunity to build influence. It could lead to a situation where you coach them, or it could just be you sharing a little advice. Either way, you've begun to have an impact in the area in which you improved yourself.

> If standard of living is your goal, quality of life almost never goes up. But if quality of life is your goal, your standard of living almost always goes up.
> —Zig Ziglar

6. Bring Mentees Along

As you go along in the journey, find people who are just a step behind you. Continuing the personal fitness analogy, you could find mentees in this area. Don't try to impose this on anyone, but invite people who ask you about fitness to work out with you, or go on a diet with you.

A mentee gives you feedback about your calling: If you get five mentees and cannot make progress with any of them, maybe this isn't the way you're meant to impact the world. That would be like a science teacher who can't get their students to care about or understand a concept like gravity.

This is also a way to deeply influence someone authentically. Don't think about inspiring the masses at first; just find one or two people who want similar results to what you have. You don't have to be the Jedi master with everything figured out either. You only need to be a step or two ahead of your students.

This goes for almost any setting. It could look like starting a book study group about becoming better husbands with a group at work. It might look like volunteering at a nonprofit for youths after school. Maybe it means having a formal mentorship, meeting with a younger professional every week to coach them through what you've learned so far. Pick one or two ideas and experiment with them. Review the results and revise the plan as you go. As I like to say, it's easier to steer a car once it's in motion. The same goes for your plan. Get some momentum going, *then* make changes as your vision becomes more clear.

7. Focus On Each Role You Have

We talked about the myriad roles we play in our lives, as fathers, husbands, employees, mentors, and the like. As you grow your impact in the world, don't overly focus on one of these roles. The reason

Melvin Maxwell is such a good example is that he didn't neglect his marriage or children as he worked as a pastor. He raised two healthy and successful boys while overseeing hundreds of churches. He struck a balance between the roles he needed to play, and he showed up day in and day out, investing that 1 percent each time.

So, remember to have date night while you climb the corporate ladder. Remember to invest in your career while you go to sports games for the kids. Don't neglect your spiritual and emotional life while working on your marriage. It may seem like these are all too much, but you'd be surprised how much they flow together when you bring focus and intentionality to them. For example, improvement in your spiritual life will help you become a better husband, father, and employee. Excelling in your career will free up time and flexibility for your children (as long as you don't get addicted to work).

Putting the Picture Together

When you invest in yourself, and you invest in others, two things start to happen. You begin to develop your influence, and you begin to impact the world. That's the thesis of part 1, right here at the end.

Remember, the currency for investing in yourself and others is your time. It's a finite resource that must be carefully managed. Where you place your time is where you place your value. So, make sure you value yourself enough to grow, clarify your passions, and begin to look outward. The overflow of investing in yourself will lead to investment in others. This will identify your calling much more clearly than, say, a weekend vision retreat.

Developing an influence is as simple as leading yourself and others. Keep other people's interests in mind, and watch as your calling becomes even clearer. Experiment and learn by doing, and start small. Over time, you'll find yourself impacting the world. It's about giving that 1 percent with a good attitude consistently. Do this in each of your plethora of roles, and get more and more specific with your investments as you go. All of these combined will give you as clear an image of your calling as you can get.

Now, how do you live out that calling? It involves how you steward your time, talents, and treasure . . .

Chapter Summary

Impacting the world is a natural by-product of developing your influence. It is usually passive and indirect instead of active and direct, though sometimes you will be able to see your impact clearly. You don't need to become a larger-than-life figure like a John C. Maxwell to have a big impact either. It simply takes investing with compound interest in mind.

You have the ability to make the world a little bit better than yesterday. Focus up. Bring a positive attitude into everything you do. You can and will make the difference for people, whether they let you know about it or not. Improve yourself in the way you want the world to improve, and bring people along with you when they ask you about it. Very soon, you'll find yourself with a clearly defined calling (that will also evolve with you over time).

Key Takeaways

- Remove excuses from your vocabulary and think of one or two small ways to invest in the world.
- As you go, get more specific with the things you try. Learn by trial and error.
- Improve yourself in the way you want to see the world improved, in every arena of your life.

Part 2:

The Pieces: The "Loops and Sockets" Needed to Live Out Your Calling

What do you think about when you think of the word "steward"? Take a minute to think about your personal definition of the word.

It's a bit of an old-timey word, when you think about it. It doesn't come up much in modern times. However, I consider it to represent a wise mindset that has been mostly lost in our day and age. It defines the role we need to play when it comes to all of our "stuff" if we want to live out our calling with purpose, integrity, and excellence.

Classically, a steward is simply a person in charge of supplies, arrangements, and other people's property. A flight attendant can be considered a steward. So can a college football water boy. To me, the word reminds me of a butler or administrator, taking care of some rich person's property while they're away or otherwise engaged. I think that's the best way to look at it, when we consider the nature of reality.

If you think about it, none of your stuff is really your stuff. When people say, "I don't have the time for that," or "I'll make time for you," they don't really possess that time. They just dictate their position in space, attitude, and intentions during that specific time slot. The same goes for any talents we have. Many of our talents come as a consequence of our birth and upbringing rather than anything special we did. Plus, in terms of calling, the best way to use any talent is to give it away, symbolically transferring ownership of the gift. Lastly, our money—or treasure—isn't really ours either. If that were true, we'd be able to take it with us when we pass away.

So, we find ourselves with time, talents, and treasure, none of which are fully ours, and none of which we'll get to hold on to forever. Our job is to steward them in a way that influences and impacts the world for the better. By taking the mindset of a steward, we can hold on to our time, talents, and treasure more loosely, and think of them as important tools to leverage toward a positive vision—instead of trying to hoard them. This empowers us to live out our calling of Inspired Living.

That's what this section is all about. We'll take a chapter on time, talents, and treasure respectively, and discuss the ways we can master their use. These are the loops and sockets we need to live out our calling.

We will break down these pieces and how to use them into three chapters:

- Mastering Your Time
- Honing Your Talents
- Aligning Your Treasure

Chapter 5:

Mastering Your Time

· · · · · · · · · · · · · · · ·

To know if you're being a good steward of what God has given you, you just have to look at two things: your calendar and your checkbook.
—Marcus Hall

don't like New Year's resolutions. There, I said it.

Now, I don't mind the idea of people setting ambitious goals for themselves, or wanting to change their lives for the better. That's not what it's about. I'm all for that. However, I don't like the success rate of New Year's resolutions. They never seem to pan out, at least for most people.

I'll give an example. Many people like to go to the gym to work out multiple times a week. They're "regulars." But gym regulars often hate going to the gym in January. That's when everyone who has decided they want to change their health and fitness comes in and signs up for a membership, and then begins using all the machines. Everyone has a hard time getting their workout done when the gym is so packed like that.

However, the regulars know they never have to wait long. While the gym feels crowded in January, by mid-February they can always get the workout machine they need, without having to wait at all. In these six weeks, the gym will go from overflowing to the same as before. Only the regulars are left. Why does this happen?

For one, we're enamored by the idea of overnight success and big change. We watch movies where a hero goes through a transformation in the span of one three-minute montage, not realizing that true change requires much more time than that. We see people win the lottery, or go viral on the internet, and suddenly their life is completely different. These ideas are attractive, but they're not real.

The same exact principle applies when it comes to time management. We want the magic productivity app. We follow seventeen blogs about time management, only to realize we've wasted two hours reading tips that we won't incorporate into our lives. We think that if we arrange our to-do list in a certain way, we'll get everything done and feel amazing while doing it.

While there's nothing wrong with productivity tools (I use a few myself), there is something wrong with this mindset. We're looking in the wrong place for our solution to time. Believe it or not, good time management is a bit of a misnomer. We can't master our time through good time management principles. We actually master it through focus management and energy management.

Why? Because unless you're Marty McFly, you can't control time at all. You have no influence over the seconds passing by as you read the words on this page. You do, however, have some influence over your focus and over your energy (because we can't really manage time, if you think about it). If you learn how to invest those correctly, you can steward your time well.

Marcus Hall: Time Management

Marcus Hall is a financial advisor who helps clients make decisions about their long-term financial goals, including retirement, and helps them connect these goals to their everyday life.

Time management is one of those things that everyone thinks about, yet so few of us get right. Without it, I see folks burning oil and spinning the hamster wheel, but once they figure it out, they start to move forward in their business, family, and everything. Today, I want to break down three big principles that will give your time management a massive overhaul.

First, though, we need to review what I call the "Two Big Cs." If you want to be a good steward of the time God's given you, look at two things: your calendar and your checkbook. If you know where you spend your time and money, you'll really know what's important in your life.

Number one, discipline. Scripture repeatedly tells us how important discipline is in everything—productivity, parenting, wealth, and more. As e 10:4 writes, "A slack hand causes poverty, but the hand of the diligent makes rich" (ESV). Without discipline, time slips away and money vanishes. But with it, you'll be in control of both.

Number two, objectives. What gets people into trouble is looking at the scoreboard too often. If you keep reminding yourself that your team is down two touchdowns, that doesn't help anybody. Instead, a key to time management is setting smaller, achievable objectives along the way. Catch the pass, make it to first down, repeat. That's how you make progress in managing your time.

Number three, do the right thing over and over. Remember *The Tortoise and the Hare?* It's an insightful book because it's true. The hare wanted to cut corners to win, but he ran out of gas as a result. Time and time again, I see folks trying to do too much at once, trying to get out of debt too fast, and they cause more trouble for themselves. Meanwhile, the tortoise chose to do the right thing, slow and steady over and over, and he won because of it. That's what I tell everyone I work with: Put the shovel down and stop digging a bigger hole, first. You didn't get into the hole overnight, so you're not going to get out of it overnight.

Focus Management

Our world tries to pull our attention in one million different directions every day. Don't quote me on that; it's not a scientifically derived number. But it certainly feels that way, doesn't it? The problem is, we can only focus on one thing at a time. This is an irrefutable fact that half of you are about to try to refute.

You might say, "Thanks, Scott, but I'm actually pretty good at multitasking. This means I don't need to listen to your advice on focus management." To that, I would say this: I didn't say anything about multitasking. I only talked about multifocusing. No human being in history has ever been multifocused. They've only shifted their focus frequently and deliberately enough to accomplish multiple tasks at relatively the same time. However, you cannot focus on multiple things at the same time. This is where it becomes exceptionally important to manage (and steward) our focus.

Are you paying attention to the things most aligned with your calling from day to day? Or, do you find yourself getting distracted by news, politics, social media, or the latest gossip at work?

If spending time with your family is high on your priority list, do you actually spend time with them? Also, when you are with them, are you actually with them? Sometimes we think we're spending quality time with our loved ones, but really, we're looking at our phone, or thinking about our next day of work, or worrying about something.

Consider your goals. We all want to develop our influence and impact the world in some way. For some people, this might mean growing their business by 100x. For others, it might mean raising several healthy and relatively well-adjusted children.

Whatever your goal, answer honestly: Are you spending time in growth activities directly related to your goal?

I'm not talking about maintenance activity, but growth activity. For example, if you want to land bigger clients at your job, you need to focus on reaching them and speaking their language. That's a growth activity. Performing work for existing clients is maintenance.

The same goes with family. Putting food on the table and showing up to big school events is maintenance. Growth would look like pursuing a special hobby with them or taking the time to learn something new about them.

Find alignment between your goals and your focus. When I coach somebody new, this is where most of their problems can be traced back to. They want a larger business, but they aren't actually focused on growing it. They want better finances, but they are afraid to look at them. That's like trying to build a puzzle using pieces from the wrong box—it just won't work.

So, don't think in terms of time management but focus management. That's the first half of the battle. The second half has to do with our energy.

Energy Management

We all get twenty-four hours in a day. That's 168 hours in a week. It's an even playing field for every person who has ever existed. However, we don't have even energy levels, or an even spread of what restores or diminishes our energy. I'm not talking about physical or electrical energy here, for the most part. I'm talking about emotional energy.

Different activities drain our energy, and others increase our energy. Have you noticed that after certain meetings or work activities, you feel spent? Have you also noticed that your favorite hobby or a conversation with your best friend can leave you buzzing? Even though those activities drain physical energy, they leave us in a different emotional state. It's a different set of batteries to charge, and not always one we pay attention to.

For one, we need to learn how to keep our batteries charged. Instead of thinking in terms of time management, we need to think of our energy levels. If we lead a lifestyle that consistently drains our emotional energy, we'll end up feeling stressed out, and maybe even burn out. It will certainly begin to affect our physical health, job performance, and relationships after a while. This is part of why we need vacations and sabbaticals every so often, but more than that, we ought to live each week in a way that promotes energy instead of depleting it.

Take a look at your weekly schedule and pay attention to what adds and what subtracts energy. Some people find it helpful to write out a physical agenda and put a plus, minus, or equals sign next to each activity to denote an increase, decrease, or even balance of energy, respectively. You can also add up every hour of your week using a +1, a -1, and a 0 for each hour, and see what balance you're left with. This gives you a rough idea of whether your week promotes energy.

Some people will realize that they need to schedule more fun in their lives. They need time by themselves for creative or intellectual pursuits. They also need time with their most essential relationships, like date nights or hangouts. Organize your week to give you a positive charge on most weeks.

Other people might see that they actually have a surplus of energy. They aren't challenging themselves to go after their goals. In this way, they don't steward their energy to line up with their calling either. They need to add moments where they do the hard and necessary work to see improvement in the most vital arenas of life.

Finally, energy can be used as a fantastic barometer. A job that aligns with our calling will fan the flame and make us feel energized when we work in it. Of course, we will always find some tasks unpleasant or unfavorable, but they won't rob us of our energy on a deep level. It's like me with public speaking. Whenever I speak in front of a crowd, I often feel physically tired and like to take a nap afterward. However, I feel more positive emotional energy. The act of public speaking lifts my soul up, in a way.

So, when we manage our focus and energy correctly, we'll begin filling our weeks with activities that feed our soul while moving us toward our best influence and impact. You might feel like you have a full schedule when you do this, but you won't feel like any of it is going to waste. Now that's proper time management.

Productivity Culture Is Broken

The problem with most educational content centered around productivity is simple: they only talk to about 25 percent of the population.

Have you ever heard of DISC? This is a personality assessment tool focused quite a bit toward the workplace, but one which I find incredibly helpful for everyone I coach. In the DISC, you have four main styles: Dominance, Influence, Steadiness, and Conscientiousness.

People with a **Dominance** style, which I prefer to call **Drivers**, are results-focused. They don't need a seventy-two-page manual before they get to work on a project. However, they can be easily distracted or overpower other people with their force of personality. Oftentimes, results are more important than relationships.

People with an **Influence** style are socially focused. They prefer to work in groups and make sure people feel seen and heard.

However, they battle with disorganization and impulsivity. They prize affirmation and energy, sometimes over the hard truth.

Steadiness types focus on stability. They like to keep the peace and support others. However, they might struggle to find their own voice or avoid confrontation. They might value the status quo over necessary change.

Lastly, we have the **Conscientious** folks. They focus on accuracy. They love to follow checklists and assure quality. On the other hand, they can be too critical of themselves and others. They might stick to a broken process because "it's the right thing to do," even when there's an exception.

You might already have an idea of what your type is. They all have their strengths, weaknesses, and defining characteristics. The problem is, productivity management content mostly only speaks to C-type people. After all, they're the ones who are most likely to keep a meticulous calendar and actually perform everything on their to-do list every day. I personally can't relate!

So, as we discuss time management (not to mention talents and treasure), it's important to contextualize the teaching in terms of the individual personality reading it. I don't want to teach you the wrong thing for you, because my advice is only best for one type on the DISC. That's also why I've discussed focus and energy management instead of time management. Time management tips are well and good, but only a minority of people will take them and run with them. However, everyone can begin thinking about how they steward their focus and energy given their unique personality.

The thing that ties it all together, regardless of DISC style, is our habits.

Habits

> The tortoise wins every time. By doing the right things over time,
> slow and steady wins the race.
> **—Marcus Hall**

Not every personality is wired for conscientious time management protocols, but every single human being has habits. Thus, if we want to crack the code on time management, we have to become intentional and deliberate about our daily, weekly, monthly, and yearly habits. When we integrate a habit into our life, it actually hacks the time management process.

First, when a task is a habit, it takes far less time to perform than when it's unusual or new. Second, our habits are so ingrained in us that it actually takes no focus on our part to perform them. How often have we gotten out of bed, brushed our teeth, made coffee, and gone out the door while thinking about something besides our immediate task the entire time? Probably every day!

Lastly, our habits take far less emotional energy to perform, even the ones that are difficult in the moment, like exercise. When it isn't a habit, we often worry about whether we'll exercise, entertain that mental debate, spend time dreading it, and waste energy looking for our workout shoes since we haven't jogged in a while. However, if it's an automatic habit, we'll find ourselves out on the sidewalk running before we even realize what's happening to us.

If we actually took the time to recognize and write out everything we do habitually, we'd probably end up with five or six pages full of tasks—and that's just Monday. Making the bed. Brushing our teeth. Showering. Getting dressed. Making coffee. Packing lunch. Tying our shoelaces. Driving to work. Walking to our office. Checking our email. Attending a meeting. Hitting the drive-through on the way home. Checking our phone. Streaming a show. Pouring ourselves a glass of wine. The list goes on and on.

Each habit can be further divided into subhabits as well. Take driving, for instance. Buckling your seatbelt is a habit. Shifting gears at certain intervals is a habit. Following red and green lights is a habit. Checking our mirrors is a habit. Yelling at someone when they cut you off is a habit. If we've been driving for any length of time, we do some or all of these, all without thinking.

Habits themselves are value-neutral; keep that in mind. I don't buy into the idea of "bad habits" and "good habits." For the most part, the act of performing most of these tasks isn't right or wrong. So, there's no need to feel guilty if we don't have the set of habits we want.

However, the results we get from our habits can be good or bad—or, at least, preferable or not preferable. The obvious example would be a salad habit versus a burger and fries habit. If that meal was dinner every day, what sort of results would you get after a few months?

The simple and hard truth is, if we want a different result, we need a different habit. It's not a deep and mystical answer; it just feels hard-to-reach because of how difficult it can be. There is almost nothing harder in life than removing bad habits and retaining good habits, and I wish it was the other way around.

Thankfully, we have a process for this, which we'll dive into for each pillar of Inspired Living: time, talent, and treasure.

But first, a mind shift.

We Need to Be More Intentional than Ever

A life unexamined is not worth living.

—Socrates

I think Socrates was onto something here. We want to examine our lives, especially the way we spend our time, if we want to live out our calling and impact the world. This requires something I call intentionality. Intentionality means that whatever you do, you do it deliberately. You do it on purpose.

It means that everything on your calendar should be examined, and serve an overall purpose for how you steward your time on earth. If something doesn't line up with your ideas about your calling, then you have to remove it. Additionally, it involves brainstorming the habits and activities that promote passion and growth and deliberately ensuring they have a space on the calendar.

Out of the three (time, talents, and treasure), time might be the most difficult one to pay attention to. You can see the numbers in your bank account and investment portfolio. You have a good idea of the kinds of skills you have, or at least the ones you want. But time is invisible. It keeps on slippin', slippin', slippin' into the future, as Steve Miller would say. And you don't get a single millisecond back.

Money and talent have the potential to increase as you go through life. Time is always decreasing. However, it doesn't really feel like it! Only when we look back at our lives do we often realize how fast it's going. Because time is always becoming scarcer, that means it's the most valuable resource you have. That's why I talked about how it's the best currency for investing in yourself and others. We have to mindfully and intentionally steward our focus, energy, and habits to get the most out of the finite time we have. Fortunately, there's some good news:

A New (Iterative) Process

In chapter 3, I mentioned that finding your calling is iterative. What that means is that you can take small steps forward and shift as you go. The same goes for stewarding our time, treasure, and talents. That's why I want to share a process that we'll continually revisit throughout this section.

Keep your ideas about the DISC in mind as we go through this process, by the way. Some personalities will feel drawn to planning, and others will want to push past it. Some will want to execute all day long, while others would prefer to talk things through a bit more. Lean into the areas that challenge you, and don't spend too long in the areas you feel complacent.

1. Plan

While plans do change, and the best-laid ones often go awry, we still need them. They provide a template for us to walk forward into the unknown. Heck, sometimes they even work out the way we draw them up.

In terms of time, we need to plan our years and months, but especially our weeks. A week is enough time to get something done, see a small-but-true result, and avoid flukes. Your average week will determine the outcome of your life. So, plan it. Cook up your ideal week in your mind, and begin aligning your focus and energy in that direction. What habits do you need to pick up to aid the process? Which bad habits are holding you back?

2. Execute

While plans help, you actually have to do the work. How many of us have written "Go to the gym" on our agenda or calendar and found ourselves at an entirely different location when that time slot came up? There is no substitute for good old-fashioned action.

For time, it requires sticking to the tasks we place on our calendar. We need to push through energy-draining tasks and savor energy-increasing ones. If we need to form a good habit, we need to intentionally make room for it every single day. Nike put it best with their motto "Just Do It."

3. Review

Remember the part about living an examined life? This is where it comes into play. We need to pay attention to what happens. This could mean setting up a weekly reflection time. It also looks like tracking and capturing the results of our activities.

If we want to steward our time well, we need to reflect on how we invested it over the course of the week. Take stock of what our calendar said, and what we actually did. You could create a daily schedule of what you expected to happen, and then leave some space beside it for what *actually happened* during those times. Additionally, keep an account of your net energy gain or loss at the end of the week, and whether you nailed your necessary habits.

4. Revise

In this stage, we think about everything that happened during the trial run and reflect on it. What went well, and what went poorly? We also take the time to reconnect our activities with our overall "why," so we understand the benefits and consequences of succeeding or failing.

For time, this means adjusting the plan based on the previous week's results. It doesn't mean changing absolutely everything every week either! In science, we prefer to focus on as few variables as possible at one time. So, change the plan to include the one habit you need to add or the one energy-draining activity you need to delegate.

5. Repeat

In the scientific method, we can't draw any conclusions unless we can repeat the experiment under the same conditions. This is why the process for Inspired Living is iterative. We run a nearly-unlimited number of trials through our lives, improving a tiny bit each time.

So, live the next week. Try to live it in as much alignment with your calling as possible. Take into account what you learned and what you revised. Continue gathering data. Remain curious. You'll start to see a tiny bit of progress, which will motivate you for the next trial. Happy experimenting!

Specific Strategies

Some personalities will want to know the main process (which I outlined above) and get going. Others will want more details. Different strategies below will appeal to you depending on your own personality.

I recommend taking one or two and adding them to your iterations. And if you want help, I created resources for each of these strategies to help you take action. Just visit InspiredLivingBook. com to download them.

1. Understand Yourself

Knowing the way you think about time is a fantastic place to start. Some people lose track if it's passing quickly, while others find themselves watching the time go by instead of executing. This is one place that taking a formal DISC assessment or working with a coach can help you tremendously. It will identify the strengths you bring to time management and the pitfalls you need to navigate.

2. Perform the Fifteen-Minute Miracle

If you are a detail-oriented person, this one's for you. Take a sheet of paper and write out your entire schedule in fifteen-minute increments, for the entire day. Even write things like driving, using social media, and eating food. Then, set your phone to make a ding or vibrate whenever the fifteen-minute increment is met. At this point, immediately shift to whatever's next on the list.

I guarantee you'll get more done and notice more opportunities with this little miracle. You'll find yourself wasting less time, and even thinking about what you need to do next, less. This is because work tends to fill the time we allow for it. If we give ourselves two hours to make a couple of phone calls and answer our email, we will take that amount of time. But if we only give ourselves fifteen minutes, we will take *that* amount of time. By the way, you could also try this with ten- or thirty-minute increments and find what suits you best.

3. Get 1 Percent Better Every Day

This one appeals to the big-picture thinkers out there. We did the math in the last chapter: If you improve at something 1 percent every day, then in three months, you'll be 245 percent better. Don't get lost in the details; just make a small investment in your improvement. Change one small item on your calendar, get five minutes faster at a task, spend thirty seconds finding a few things to be grateful for before you walk in your door in the evening, things like that. It will pay dividends.

4. Budget Your Time

For some, it may make sense to budget your time like it is actually money. Some of us find budget spreadsheets and bank statements easy to understand and manipulate. If that's you, take advantage of it. You need to budget 168 hours every week. Some tasks are like your expenses: you simply need to do them. This includes sleeping a healthy amount, by the way! However, other tasks are like your luxuries. You don't necessarily need them, but they are very nice to have and include. Thinking of your time in this way could help you steward it more effectively.

5. Create Routines

Not everyone wants to write out their day in fifteen-minute chunks. Some people know that if they have a solid start to their day, they'll feel unstoppable for the rest. This is known as "getting up on the right side of the bed." If that's you, write out how you will begin and end every day. Then, improvise the middle part.

By the way, this could also mean making a work startup and work shutdown routine. Very few people I've met actually do this, but it helps tremendously. If you develop a set of actions you perform at the end of your shift (e.g., shut down the computer, take a deep breath, change out of my uniform, put on a different hat), you'll feel more present in your next environment.

6. Get to Inbox Zero

This is a tough one, especially for people who don't read their emails as often as they should. Inbox Zero simply means ending each workday with zero unread emails in your inbox. Everything has been dealt with, even if that means moving it straight to the trash or unsubscribing. I'm telling you it's possible because I do it myself. Getting to Inbox Zero feels like one less cluttered space in my life and in my mind, which promotes both energy and focus.

Remember, I created resources for each of these strategies to help you take action. Just visit InspiredLivingBook.com to download the resources I created to help you.

No More New Year's Resolutions

> I really believe that different parts of your life can thrive when something starts going right and you're proactive in that place. Doing this can bring all your ships on a rising tide.
>
> **—Marcus Hall**

Remember, you'll get better at mastering your time . . . over time. If you make small changes each week, and follow the iterative process, you'll see a world of difference—it will just take a few weeks before it is all measurable. This is a far more reliable way to improve your time management (and therefore, life) than New Year's resolutions.

Don't be like the people who try to change everything at once and then burn themselves out trying. I want to see you next to me at the exercise machine on February 16, and beyond. This requires understanding your personality and how you'll relate to the iterative process I outlined. Then, it means incorporating the specific strategies that resonate with you most, both consistently and over time.

Steward your focus. Steward your energy. Steward your habits. When you put these together, you'll find yourself mastering your time.

Chapter Summary

The way we think about time management as a culture is flawed. First of all, most productivity hacks only work for really conscientious people who love lists and detailed plans. Second, nobody can really "manage" time at all. The best we can do is steward our focus and steward our energy in ways that line up with our calling.

This all has to do with our habits. If we can do something without thinking about it, or even spending much energy on it, and we know it leads to a good result, then we're well on our way. This mindset will enable us to go beyond the New Year's resolution culture and into authentic growth.

Key Takeaways

- Determine how your personality views time, agendas, and schedules. Do you love to keep detailed lists, or do you prefer to just get to work?
- Follow the iterative process when it comes to mapping out your weeks: Plan, Execute, Review, Revise, Repeat.
- Consider which specific strategies are right for your personality, and try one or two for yourself.

Chapter 6:

Honing Your Talents

．　．　．　．　．　．　．　．　．　．　．　．　．

I magine you get invited to a game show where they give away fabulous prizes for random contests. Maybe there are fifteen other contestants, and a few of you get knocked out of the competition each round. The last person to successfully pass every challenge? They get $1,000,000.

In round one, you manage to spin five plates on sticks at once, holding one with each limb and another balanced on your forehead. Well done! Five other contestants get knocked out. Then, you have five tries to hit a perfect kickflip on a skateboard. Though it takes you a moment to knock off the rust, you eventually hit the perfect flip on try five and the studio audience goes wild. Another six contestants couldn't shred like that, so they get eliminated.

Then, the charismatic host explains the final challenge. He says you need to balance on one foot, in direct competition with the other four contestants. Whoever remains balanced the longest wins the grand prize. During the contest, the floor might shake a little, maybe a clown comes and sprays water on you, and to top it off, let's say a wind machine turns on intermittently and attempts to blow you over.

What's your strategy? How do you win this simple contest? I'll tell you what I would do. At the start of the competition, I would lift one of my legs, choose a fixed place on the wall to stare, and then zone out. I would keep staring at my target with white-hot intensity, regardless of what distractions came. If my competition doesn't do the same, they'll eventually fall over because of the distractions, resistance, and plain old lack of balance. Then I'd take a nice long vacation with my $1,000,000.

The moral of the story is, balance is much easier when you have a fixed target. When I think about honing talents, I think about all the talents necessary to function in life. These are the skills needed for showing up at work, in your marriage, for your family, for your church . . . and not to mention, your personal health and finances. We have a wide range of areas we need to develop skills in, and as we learned in the last chapter, limited time, focus, and energy.

That's why we need to develop a fixed target that stays relatively the same on our horizon. This will enable us to have balance—and more than that, it will show us which skills we need to learn next.

Stephanie Scheller: Contentment and Self-Awareness

Stephanie Scheller is an entrepreneur and marketer who works with multiple events companies. These events teach business owners how to market their businesses and business people with ADHD how to thrive in their careers.

As an entrepreneur, there's no skill more crucial than self-awareness. Why? Because self-awareness shows you where you are and where you need to go. Without it, you'd be shocked at how quickly you can find yourself off-course or spinning the hamster wheel. We live in a culture saturated with success stories, but each person got to where they are because they practiced and refined self-awareness. So if you're itching to build something, here are some self-awareness principles that have served me and my clients:

First off, you're not as good as you think you are. The problem is, when we're a little bit better than most people at something, we tend to think we're really good at something. That doesn't mean we are! Instead, take an honest assessment of where you are and go from there. Once you realize you're at Level 1, you can work your way to Level 2.

Second, avoid being a commodity. When entrepreneurs don't know themselves well enough, they can't differentiate themselves from their competition. Once that happens, they become a commodity, which means fighting for the lowest price. Don't do it! If you want to go beyond price, your consumers have to feel like they're getting something beyond what you offer. Self-awareness is the key to doing that.

Finally, the journey to success is long, so be content with where you are. We hear all about these "overnight success stories," but in reality, most "overnight successes" took forty years! That's why it's imperative that you cultivate contentment in your work—that's the key to appreciating your progress while driving growth. Don't rush your success!

What Does "Talent" Mean?

You see, talent has a much broader definition than "what you happen to be good at." We might be tempted to think of talents like a high school talent show, where one kid tries to juggle, and another sings their favorite karaoke song. The way I view talent goes beyond this narrow definition.

I'll try to put it as simply as possible: Talent is what you're doing, and what you're not doing. You get good at doing what you're doing, and you also get good at not doing what you're not doing. I know that sentence probably broke all the rules of grammar, but it's true.

You get good at what you're doing. Human beings have a remarkable capacity to learn and grow. Even if it doesn't feel like it, we will gain skill over time in everything we do—though the progress may feel too slow to really detect. However, if we bring a level of intentionality (there's that word again) into it, we can find ourselves developing our skills and talents much faster than previously expected.

You also get good at not doing what you're not doing. I chose those words on purpose. I didn't say, "Your skills depreciate over time," or "You'll never get good at something if you don't practice it," even though those statements are true and worth considering. I'm adding a level to it, however: If you don't do something, you will actually become skilled at not doing it. For example, many people are very skilled at not getting up on time. Put differently, they are skilled at hitting the snooze button or playing out a mental debate about whether they should really get up and exercise or just sleep in.

Therefore, not only do we grow in the tasks we perform, but also the ones we avoid. That's why it can be so difficult to change someone once they are set in their ways and have lived a long time. They have become very skilled at doing X, but also very skilled at not doing Y.

Now, depending on what you fill in the variable with, the person could be fine. Maybe they are very skilled at their job and also very skilled at not making excuses. On the other hand, you could have the opposite situation. Perhaps they are very skilled at doing the bare minimum and also very skilled at not taking responsibility for their actions.

Are you starting to see how this works? You invest in talent through both action and inaction because, if you think about it, inaction is still a form of action. At least, that's what the laws of physics tell us. It's the concept of potential energy. Every object has some degree of energy due to its relative position in space, positive or negative electrical charge, and perhaps most relevant to us, internal stresses.

This energy persists even when the object isn't moving. Even as you sit in a chair, gravity is pushing the chair into your behind, and your behind is pushing back with equal force. Otherwise, one of you would be pushing the other.

Okay, I get it, enough science lessons. What does this mean for honing our talents, living out our calling, and impacting the world?

It means we have to pay exceptionally close attention to what we're doing, and what we're not doing. Plus, we have to bring deliberate attention to the skills that need to be increased or decreased. However, none of these skills (or lack thereof) will matter unless we have the right target. So, we need to learn how to distinguish between our assignment, purpose, and calling, and fix our eyes on the correct point in the horizon. This eventually gives us momentum in our pursuit of influencing others and impacting the world. But first . . .

Here's a Little Secret about Talent

In my time coaching people toward Inspired Living, I've noticed a pattern. In the helping professions, it might be called the "presenting problem" or "presenting issue." Most people have a presenting problem when they begin working with me, which makes sense. Very few people hire a coach when they think everything is going well and they're meeting their potential.

However, I've noticed that the presenting problem almost always falls into one of two categories. It nearly always has to do with time or treasure. People say, "I feel like I don't have enough time to accomplish everything I want to, while being a good dad." Or they say, "I know I can change careers and grow my business, but I just don't know how to get there."

Any good coach will tell you, however, that the presenting problem often isn't the real problem. It's like a patient going to the doctor's office because they feel tired all the time, only to find out they have sleep apnea.

The real problem usually involves talents, not time or treasure. In fact, the majority of work I do with people I coach has to do with talents, even when they mostly come wanting something to do with time or treasure. That's because the right talents—in other words, getting good at doing the right things and not doing the wrong things—will always lead to one feeling better about their time and treasure situation.

Let me put it this way: How you handle your time and money is all about how you handle *yourself*. And that has to do with our skills. Remember how I said time management was a bit of a misnomer? It's really about managing your focus and energy, right? Well, managing your focus and energy are forms of managing yourself. At the end of the day, you need to manage yourself well if you want to manage time well.

So, we can't always directly change our time or money situation, but we can change ourselves. We can get better at managing ourselves. We can learn self-discipline, lower distractibility, increase our willpower, implement systems and processes, and of course, develop good habits. This all falls under the talent domain.

Now, you might say, "That's all well and good, but the problem really is that I'm not making enough money." I'd say, you're probably right. However, even there, if you have the right mindset, attitude, and approach, you'll get out of "brokeness" really quickly.

There's a difference between broke and poor. One has to do with our mindset, and the other has to do with our circumstances. That's why when I coach people toward proper money or time management, they'll often say, "I feel like I got a raise!" or "I have so much more time now," even if their bank account is the same and they still have the same twenty-four hours as the rest of us. The only difference? They've started to pay attention, and they've begun to manage themselves.

Plus, they tend to lose weight! Almost all of my coaching clients report better outcomes in their physical health, even if that's not what we've been talking about at all. It's because discipline in one area of life tends to bleed over into other areas. Why? Because you're paying attention.

We Need to Perform Difficult Self-Examination

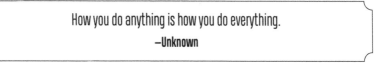

How you do anything is how you do everything.
—Unknown

Have you heard that quote before? A friend of mine likes to tweak it and tell me, "How you do anything meaningful is how you do everything meaningful." Because let's face it, how you tie your shoelaces, or the order you put your shoes on in, probably doesn't matter in the long run. I'm willing to be wrong on this, but so far, I haven't heard of anyone gaining their dream job because they cut their ham sandwich diagonally instead of horizontally.

However, the meaningful things we do certainly affect each other. I think it's because they have to do with how we learn. See, when we learn a new skill, we shouldn't just pay attention to how to perform that skill, but also how we learn it. In other words, "improving our skills" is a skill in itself! To get better at getting better will require intense self-examination and reflection. It's hard work. It's also uncomfortable.

This process tends to reveal baggage. We can't operate in a mode of intense self-examination without finding a few skeletons in the closet. It will feel difficult to accept times in the past when we have run away from our calling or acted in a way misaligned with it. It will show us just how far we are from our target.

However, even though the process is difficult, it leads to benefits across every area of life. If we get better at getting better, then we'll learn every skill we need more quickly. This will have a compounding effect on our lives. It starts with gut-wrenching honesty, however.

What are you currently doing that's in alignment with your calling? What are you currently doing that doesn't line up? What are you not doing that you should be doing? What are you not doing that you should continue not doing? The answers to these four questions will reveal the set of skills you need to learn—or unlearn.

But wait, you might ask, how do we determine our target in the first place?

Now's a Good Time to Bring Up Ikigai

> What I found is that almost all people are
> "forty years overnight" success stories.
> —Stephanie Scheller

We talked about how our calling reveals itself through investing in ourselves, and others, and developing our influence right where we're at. We also talked about how our calling reveals itself through the fire (passion) and the feedback we get as we go. Now, I want to lay an additional framework down that may help some personality types parse what we're talking about.

It's called ikigai, which is a Japanese term meaning "a reason for being." You can get a reason for being by answering four crucial questions:

1. What do you love to do?
2. What does the world need?
3. What are you good at?
4. What can you get paid to do?

In the overlap between these four questions, you can find your reason for being. It will still be an iterative process, as the answers to those four questions can and do shift. However, it gets you started in the right direction.

I have another framework I like to use in addition to ikigai that might simplify the process even further:

1. Assignment

Simply put, your assignment is the "what," the things you're doing right now. It's your job, your responsibilities, your obligations. It's temporary and changes over time. Say your career is in the world of finance. You might have an assignment as a bank teller for a time, and then later, become a loan officer. In this instance, your calling hasn't changed, but your assignment has.

2. Purpose

At the other end of the spectrum is your purpose, your overarching theme. It's your big "why," often outlined in a positive, grandiose statement. A purpose might stay with you for your entire life without changing. Back to the finance example. Your purpose might be to help people get the most out of their money, or ensure generational wealth and stability. Regardless of what you're doing from day to day, you aim to meet that purpose in some small way through it all.

3. Calling

Your calling is the "how"; namely, how your assignment and purpose play with each other and play out. While your purpose remains the same, your calling can shift. For example, your calling will show up differently in your role as a father as opposed to your role in the finance world. The problem comes when people mix up their assignment with their calling.

For example, parenting is an assignment, by and large. If you think of parenting as your lifelong calling, what happens when your kids move out? Your role as a parent will stop being dominant in your life as your kids become adults and your authority and influence over them diminishes.

So, think of your purpose as your overall vision, your calling as your mission statement, and your assignment as your temporary roles.

Let's sum up. We've determined that honing our talents requires a fixed point on the horizon, a purpose we're moving toward. We live that purpose by discovering and operating in our calling, and it manifests itself most clearly in our assignments. All three require us to learn certain skills, in other words, the things we're doing and the things we're not doing. Discovering which skills we need to learn and unlearn requires hard self-examination, but when done well, improvement bleeds over into every area of our life. So, how do we hone our talents?

The Iterative Process Strikes Back

The same process that helps us master our time helps us hone our talents. It is the act of planning, executing, reviewing, revising, and repeating that we went over in the last chapter. Let's go through each step and talk specifically about how it relates to honing our talents.

Again, keep the DISC in mind as we go through the process. Some personalities will feel drawn to planning, and others will want to push past it. Some will want to execute all day long, while others would prefer to talk things through a bit more. Lean into the areas that challenge you, and don't spend too long in the areas you feel complacent.

Plan

Take the four questions of ikigai. Again, they are as follows:
1. What do you love to do?
2. What does the world need?
3. What are you good at?
4. What can you get paid to do?

Write down your answers for each one and note the overlap between your answers. Some people will have one concept they find for each that fits like a glove, and others will need to do more searching. Wherever you're at, that's okay.

From there, distill your purpose, calling, and assignment given the definitions above. You may find yourself in an assignment tailored to your calling or not, by the way. Regardless of where you are, you haven't reached the ultimate fixed point on the horizon yet. There are ways you need to change your assignment and shift your calling in order to reach your purpose.

That's where talents come into play. If you need a new assignment, then you need to learn new skills. You don't just show up one day and say, "I'm ready to be promoted to loan officer." You need to become the kind of person who can operate well in that role, by having the requisite talents. Or you might find that you've been neglecting part of your calling. We'll see this more clearly in the wheel exercise below. This will also show you skills you need to learn and unlearn.

Depending on your personality, take one to three skills you know you need to focus on, and start learning.

Execute

Whatever your talent, walk in it. If you need to get better at playing the drums, then play them for an hour a day, or fifteen minutes, however long you can. Skills are gained through consistent, deliberate, and adequately long practice sessions. The more of these deliberate practice sessions you have, and the longer they are, the faster you'll improve. So, book a few practice sessions into your week.

If your skill is a bit more vague, like "communication skills," part of your practice will be researching and learning how to improve it. Whatever talent you need to improve in, there is a plethora of resources available for you to tap into.

Review

Unlike time or treasure, it's often hard to quantify whether you're doing the right thing. You often have to feel it intuitively instead. This comes easier to some types than others. I recommend finding a way to record your journey so that you can see your progress. This could look like creating a practice log, keeping a diary of your sessions, or scheduling a time to talk about your progress with a loved one or mentor. These records will give you enough data to allow you to review your progress.

Revise

Be it a diary, log, or conversations with a mentor, you'll come up with changes to incorporate to grow your skill more quickly. Not only will you gain insight on ways to improve the skill, but you'll also get better at improving all skills. This is the "getting better at getting better," we talked about earlier. Lean into the modalities that help you improve more quickly as you discover them.

Repeat

It's so difficult with talents and skills to measure our improvement. With time and treasure, you can generally tell whether there's been an improvement over ninety days of time. You'll see a vast difference in a person's productivity or bank accounts.

With talents, it's tougher. In fact, you might even feel worse before you do better. That's because instead of performing the skill reflexively, you're thinking about it. When you think about something, you slow down and freeze up more easily. Plus, when you press into new ways of doing old things, you feel amateurish and inexperienced at first. It's not uncommon to get emotional during this process, or even discover dreams you've been neglecting. You might feel like you aren't far enough along yet.

That's why it's about honing. We repeat the process, again and again, discarding what isn't useful and keeping what helps us get sharper. Plus, if baggage comes up, we can unpack it. That's one of our specific strategies.

Specific Strategies

As with the last chapter, you may find certain strategies more or less relevant depending on your personality type. There's no pressure to try all of them, all the time.

I just want to include a variety in the hope that every reader will resonate with at least one of them.

As with other strategies in this book, I have created several resources to help you with each of these strategies. Just visit InspiredLivingBook.com to download the resources I created to help you.

1. Unpack the Baggage

A process of self-examination, when done with utter honesty, will reveal our cognitive biases, limiting beliefs, and a ton of baggage from our family of origin. This is all baggage we carry around in our head, affecting our reactions, and if we let it, our decisions. The first step is to accept the truth, which can honestly be the hardest part.

From there, the path could diverge depending on what you discover and how you're wired. You may need to talk to a mental health professional, or at least find a coach or mentor. It could involve writing letters of forgiveness to people in our past or writing letters to our past selves. As we do this, our general level of awareness and ability to move forward will increase.

2. Switch from Reactive to Proactive

For those who say, "Just give me one thing to do," I'll say this: Go on offense. Switch from going through life as if everything's happening to you, and start happening to life. Focus on what you can control, which is mostly just yourself. Pick a skill that you know you need to improve and go after it. Don't wait for the right job assignment to come along and fall in your lap; make it happen. Take ownership of your faults and shortcomings, and take ownership of your improvement.

3. Perform the Happiness Wheel

Another strategy I love that can help you is an exercise called the Happiness Wheel. The Happiness Wheel assesses all the arenas of our lives, such as career, financial, spiritual, physical, intellectual, family, and social domains.

It asks you to rank yourself in each of the most important parts of your life. By taking this simple exercise, you can better understand where you are in each arena and where you want to be. After taking the assessment, ask yourself which one (or two) of these areas you want to focus on.

Write down your answers, then evaluate them. Your first whack at it is probably superficial. Keep asking "How did I get here?" or "Why do I want that?" until you get to the truth. This reveals the big picture and the underlying patterns beneath it all. When you know what you want to improve on and why, and can connect it to your calling, you're on your way.

4. Ask the Airport Question

Imagine for a moment that it's five years in the future. You've just gotten off a plane and when looking around for a coffee shop to kill time, you run into an old friend. You've not seen them for five years, and they ask, "How is life treating you these days?" You reply, "*Amazing!* Life couldn't get any better." And you really mean it. They ask you, "What makes you say that?"

Sit down and write out why you would answer this way. What's happening in your life now that makes it amazing? Who are you with? What are you doing? Think about the various arenas of life.

What does your life look like in each? Remember, you are creating a dream future five years from now. Record your answers.

5. Look Back

Next, instead of looking at the future, travel to the past. Don't worry, this isn't an Ebenezer Scrooge situation.

Go back to the time when you got your first job. Then list your next job, and so on, and so forth. List out every job you've ever had, even volunteer work and internships. Then, answer these questions for each one:

- What did you do?
- When did you do it?
- What was good about it?
- What did you not like about it?

Finally, grade each job from a "1," meaning "I loved it so much that I'd do it for free," to a "5," meaning "Dear Lord, never make me do this again." This will show you the kinds of assignments you favor and the skills you need to brush up on.

6. Develop a Purpose Statement

> If you're selling without a mission, without something that's driving you beyond your product or service, you're going to go out of business.
> —Stephanie Scheller

This exercise can help deep thinkers and those with a poetic flair. Take the time to write out the perfect purpose statement for yourself. This could involve writing a hundred imperfect ones and honing the purpose statement until it's impeccable.

For example, is your purpose to profit at any cost? Probably not; that's a bad call. Is it serving the greater good? That seems better, but it isn't very specific yet. Keep crafting it until you feel proud of it and know it resonates with your heart. Now it's time to ask yourself the difficult questions:

Does your current assignment line up with this? What about your career? How about how you show up in your most important relationships? What about the way you treat your body or your bank account?

Remember, I created several resources to help you with each of these strategies. Visit InspiredLivingBook.com to download the resources I created to help you.

Gain Momentum

Remember how I said that improvement in one of these areas will lead to improvement in all areas? It's the law of inertia: the tendency of an object in motion to remain in motion until acted upon by an outside force; the tendency of an object at rest to remain at rest until acted upon by an outside force.

Yes, I know, not everyone wants a science lesson. Still, as an ex-physics teacher, sometimes I have to go there. How it relates to talents is that we can make positive momentum habitual. As we get better at getting better, all areas in our life will improve. That's also why it feels like when things are beginning to go wrong, everything is going wrong.

The opposite is also true: if you can turn any part of your life in a positive direction, it has the ability to drag other parts of your life in a positive direction.

Find that point on the horizon, and get intentional with your life to find an active balance. Pay attention. Use brutally honest self-examination. Identify your best guess at a purpose, calling, and assignment. Find the skills you need to improve on, and learn how to learn. This will give you momentum. This will hone your talents.

Chapter Summary

Whenever someone tells me they have a time or a treasure problem, it often boils down to a talent problem. If a person can learn how to manage themselves, and gain the relevant skills for their assignment and calling, they will realize they have more than enough time, and even feel like they've gotten a raise!

It comes down to paying attention and honest self-examination. This helps us determine a fixed point on the horizon to focus on, one that makes it easier for us to balance. All this gives us an idea of the skills we need to work on, and even helps us get better at improving our skills in general. And it leads to a compound effect where we see multiple areas of our life improve at once, giving us momentum.

Key Takeaways

- Take the time to answer the four questions of ikigai, and use the answers to derive your purpose, calling, and assignment. Remember, it's okay when these answers shift over time.
- Apply the plan, execute, review, revise, and repeat framework to one to three skills you need to learn or unlearn in order to align your assignment, calling, and purpose.
- Consider which specific strategies are right for you, and try one or two for yourself.

Chapter 7:

Aligning Your Treasures

· · · · · · · · · · · · · · · · ·

A few years ago, a coaching client, whom I'll call Luke, came to me worried about his finances. He'd heard I could help out in matters of stewardship, so he contacted me to help.

Sure enough, when we looked under the hood, Luke had several financial challenges we needed to address. The most painful problem for him right then was a decent amount of credit card debt carrying an astronomical interest rate.

Now you might remember me saying that time and treasure issues often boil down to talent issues. Thus, in addition to coaching him through his financial issues, I attempted to dig deeper with Luke to diagnose his underlying belief systems around money and identify the skills he needs to learn to align his treasure with his purpose. That way, I could not only help him treat the symptom (debt) of the real issue (something beneath the surface), but I could also help him solve the underlying issue too.

Like many people struggling with debt, Luke was more concerned about the debt than his underlying belief systems. He was more worried about the symptoms than the root cause.

That said, Luke was very motivated and followed our plan aggressively. He picked up some side work to earn extra cash, cut unnecessary expenses, and really pushed himself to the limit to climb out of this hole. Luke's dedication to earning extra cash was impressive. In a short amount of time, it began working.

Throughout this time, however, he was unwilling to go along with my attempts to go deeper with him. And as he started digging out of debt, he became less and less receptive to going deeper. After all, the problem was being solved, right?

Eventually, he worked himself out of debt and into a much better financial picture.

Without the debt that was causing him to be worried, Luke felt he no longer needed to work with me, and we went our separate ways.

Years later, Luke came to mind, so I decided to follow up with him, hoping the pain he felt before hiring me was strong enough to keep him from going back into debt. That said, I was worried because he hadn't addressed the issues under the surface, which I know is the only surefire way to prevent the symptoms from roaring back.

Sure enough, Luke confided in me that he had fallen back into old habits. He was relieved to hear from me, and my outreach motivated him to start another "financial crash diet" to reduce his new debt. That's one side of the coin, and I see it all too often. Now, take the story of another client of mine, whom we'll call Lando.

Lando has a similar financial situation to Luke at the outset, but a slightly different mindset. We go over his financial picture and determine that he should also find ways to cut expenses and earn additional income, but we should also work on the issues beneath the surface. Once again, Lando is unwilling to listen. Lando takes a look at his expenses, and he thinks I'm calling him to ask him to cut out lattes forever.

Let me back up a little. Lando has a tough job and very little margin in his life. One of his absolute joys is to go to the coffee shop early in the morning, before the busyness of the day begins, and order a complicated latte. Even though it might seem silly, that beverage keeps him going. It's the small joys. When Lando talks to me about his finances, he mistakenly assumes I'm attacking the latte. He thinks I'm trying to take the latte away from him, which would put him in an untenable position. So, he breaks off the coaching relationship.

By the way, that concept has even changed the way I coach when it comes to money. Instead of telling people what they should cut from the plan, I ask them what they absolutely want to keep *in* the plan. Even if it's a coffee beverage. Then, we go from there.

I share these two stories to illustrate two important points. Luke's story teaches us that treasures are not really about behavior, but about alignment. Out of everyone I've worked with to improve their financial picture, not one had an income or "outgo" problem. All of them have had an alignment problem. Most of them, like Luke, had a flawed belief structure about money that kept them in cycles. We'll break this down further in a minute.

Lando's story teaches us that people are irrational when it comes to money—and that's okay. Money actually has a human element; it's not a purely mathematical issue. Most people get intimidated by talking to money experts because they know it will expose inconsistent or irrational behaviors surrounding money. A smart financial coach will help them with their numbers. A wise financial coach will help them with their numbers *and* their heart.

Darryl Lyons: Finances Flow from Identity

Darryl Lyons is one of PAX Financial's three founders and its current CEO. He is also committed to ongoing professional development, a fact exemplified by his membership in relevant professional groups, such as the National Federation of Independent Business Owners (NFIB), C12 Group, Dave Ramsey Investment Advisory Council, and Goldman Sachs Personal Financial Management Advisory Council. Darryl's ambition is to create a legacy within people whose lives have been bettered via contact with him.

What's the secret to solidifying your finances? It's not as complicated as you think, despite what you might see online. From our perspective, God has a plan for all of our financial lives. Knowing this fact, these are some tried-and-true principles that have helped all of our clients find solid financial footing and know how to grow it into the future.

First, you need to understand who you are in order to understand your finances. What are your values? Your priorities? What are your five-year, ten-year, and twenty-five-year goals? Take some time in prayer and study to understand these aspects of yourself. The more you do, the more you'll understand how to approach your money.

Next, when we work with a family, it's a nonnegotiable that husband and wife are aligned. A marriage means two bodies joining into one, which means the finances have to combine too. If they disagree on where the money should be spent, how much they should save, etc., it'll only spell problems now and down the road. We dedicate as much time as we need to get husband and wife working toward the same goal.

Finally, we firmly believe that simplicity is the key to excelling financially. We've seen ordinary folks become millionaires from working jobs that pay $50,000/year . . . all because they knew their goals and saved in order to get there, even if it took years. In our experience, most people crave simplicity in their lives because it helps them focus on what's important. By prioritizing what matters to you, you can cut out the excess and start making strides. That's at the core of everything we do.

Don't Be Rational

Money is about alignment, and it's about underlying beliefs that trap us in undesired patterns. It's far from a math problem, even though a significant amount of math is involved. Take Lando, for example. If he spends $5 on that latte in the morning, that adds up to about $150 each month in fancy coffee. Most coaches would ask him to cut down on that expense. But if that coffee gives you joy and keeps you going, I say find another way.

Because we need to align our money with our heart, sometimes we have to let the heart win. We aren't like the Vulcans from Star Trek, operating on pure logic. We're emotional beings, and that is not only okay but good. The fact that we are emotional will give us tremendous motivation to seek that alignment.

Say you want to get better with money, so you head to the bookstore. Books contain knowledge, right? You begin searching for a self-help book that will teach you about money. Do you know what the genre will be called? "Personal Finance." That's the key. Like Lando's latte, it's deeply personal.

That's why I advise people against being rational when it comes to finances. Don't be rational. Sounds strange, right? Not really. As we learned above, there is no one-size-fits-all plan for financial health or an approach that works for all comers. This is especially true because everyone has different goals when it comes to money. Some people want to set up a predictable and comfortable (even lavish) retirement for themselves. Some want high income and low taxes now so they can travel the world while they're young. Others want to become millionaires. A few others don't really care about money at all; they just want to make sure they have enough to survive so they can pursue other things that make them feel alive. The purely rational approach won't perfectly help any of those people, because they have different hearts.

That's why I say be reasonable, not rational.

Take an approach that makes sense and makes you feel good now, rather than a purely rational approach. The rational approach is all about the numbers: If I can earn 8 percent annually on my investments here, and save 3 percent interest on my debt there, the math suggests it's a better return. But that math equation can't take into account your morning latte, or your hopes and dreams.

Some people need to live with that debt for a while and enjoy their life now. Perhaps they need a slower plan than Luke's because life is actually far better for them if they drive a newer car or have one more vacation per year. Or maybe they need a faster plan because they struggle with anxiety, and their debt is legitimately keeping them up at night. In that case, they may want to be more aggressive for a time.

See how these solutions strike a balance? The purely rational approach isn't helpful, but the purely emotional side doesn't help either. We all have a personal history, past decisions, a set of beliefs, and a range of emotions when it comes to money. If we acted 100 percent in line with our emotions, that wouldn't help either. We'd probably look a bit like Luke, following our whims and racking up debt, and then responding out of stress and punishing ourselves to get out of said debt.

After all, if personal finance was just a math problem, we'd all be debt-free, living rich and retiring with dignity. But how many people actually get there? So, we need to emphasize the "personal" aspect of personal finance . . . like comfort lattes.

> When you reduce some complexity in your life,
> you're able to see what's more important.
> —Darryl Lyons

Don't Crash

Unfortunately, we cannot simply shift our income and outgo and call it good. We're too complex for that. We have to align our treasure with our calling and purpose at the deepest level and make small habit changes over time. This is the exact opposite of a crash diet.

In chapter 5, we talked about how it's so hard to find an open workout machine at the gym in January. Everyone has begun their New Year's resolutions, 95 percent of which will fail by March (number based on my personal gym experience; your results may vary). Along with resolving to go to the gym every day and twice on Sunday, many people also opt into a crash diet. They drastically change their food for a month or two and suffer the whole time. However, they don't change their underlying relationship with food (or exercise). So, they lose a significant amount of weight in the first month, even up to thirty pounds! However, as soon as they start cheating, or get to their goal weight, it all comes tumbling down. That's the real crash.

> People start to mature when they start to say, 'Okay, I don't really care about the math. I just want my life to be simple. I want to enjoy things.'
> —Darryl Lyons

The same happens with our money, as we discovered with Luke. The person upends everything they're doing but doesn't address the underlying issue. We need to go deeper, beneath the surface. This way, next time you get out of debt or reach a financial goal, you stay there forever.

I've seen people get a HELOC (home equity line of credit) so that they can pay off the credit card, but they don't change their relationship with money. So, soon enough, they fall back, and now they have HELOC and credit card debt. We don't just want to work hard to get out of debt. We want to become the *kind of person* who is debt-free.

I've also seen people use a HELOC to open up cash flow so they can use it to attack their debt, while changing their money mindset and habits. Others decide to avoid HELOCs no matter what. What's important isn't the specific tactic we use, but the kind of person we become, and the good habits that flow out of it.

This is the difference between broke and poor, in my mind. Broke is a mindset; poor has to do with your circumstances. Someone can have millions of dollars and still be broke. In fact, I've met people like that. They think about money in terms of scarcity. Even though they live incredibly luxurious lives compared to, well, almost everyone, they feel poor. They say things like, "We don't have enough cash."

I've also met people who are poor. They have a healthy relationship to money, but they don't have a ton of it. Still, when it comes, they know how to use it in a way that aligns with their hearts. They don't let the tyranny of broke-ness rule their lives. When they do get more money, their heart will be in a place to handle it correctly. They won't crash.

Connect Your Why to Your Money

> For us, it was about walking through life with people and helping them understand who they are, what their priorities are, and what their values are.
> —Darryl Lyons

That's what this comes down to: the heart. We need our treasures to align with our calling and purpose in life. Then, we get our talents and time to connect with our money.

Does your money connect to your why? We can determine that. First, write out one of your goals with money. It could be "make $100,000 next year," or "get out of debt," or "purchase a house," or something else. Make it authentic to you. Now, answer this:

Why do you want that?

If your answer is "to get by," or "to have nice things," or "to stop feeling so stressed all the time," then you aren't going deep enough. These reasons fail to connect treasure with calling.

I'll give you an example: I want to help men live out their own calling through Inspired Living. This affects the way I earn, save, and spend. I know that I should earn money through some form of teaching, speaking, and coaching because that will directly fulfill my calling. I know that I need to save money and steward it well because I need to model the beliefs and behaviors that I teach. Lastly, I know I need to spend money on improving myself as a teacher and speaker, and be generous with money. Beyond all the basic items we reserve money for, I also make sure to invest in my calling.

Remember the concept of ikigai, the four questions we ask to help determine our purpose and calling? This concept can also help us connect our treasure with our calling.

Money and Ikigai Should Cooperate

Ikigai, your "reason for being," comes from answering these four questions:

1. What do you love to do?
2. What does the world need?
3. What are you good at?
4. What can you get paid for?

Of course, when we think of treasure, we might naturally gravitate toward #4. How can I get the right job that earns me the income I want? This is how people get stuck in jobs they don't love, or ones that don't seem to contribute to what the world needs. It's also a good way to get a job that doesn't jibe with our talents, which causes additional stress.

Not everything you do for your job (which is your assignment) needs to feed all four points of ikigai. If you have such a job, you're in an incredibly fortunate situation. Still, all four points need to be fed—and not just with your time and talents, but also with your treasure.

So, what do you love to do? Is it going to the coffee shop in the morning and enjoying that expensive latte? Make sure your money lines up with that. Whatever hobbies, ministries, or activities you perform that you love, that make you feel alive, invest in them. You should always have money set aside for them in your budgets, even if it isn't 100 percent rational.

What does the world need? This is where generosity often comes in. Not everyone can directly help a charitable cause or mission with their day job. However, nearly all of them need financial support from the outside. Additionally, consider your spending habits. Every time you spend money, you're affirming the creation and use of the product or service. Are you buying things you don't need, or don't think the world needs?

What are you good at? At one level, your job must align with your talents. At a deeper level, you need to invest your money into your talents. This could look like investing in coaching, taking seminars, or even going back to school. This way, you can generate even more income through your talents as you grow them. Some people work in a job that has nothing to do with their personal calling, even. But they use it to fund the work they are called to do for free.

Finally, yes, we need to consider what we can get paid for. Though ideally, we love what we do so much that we would do it for free, we also have bills. So, we need to make sure we have earnings coming from somewhere, even if it doesn't feed the other three points of ikigai. Additionally, we need to spend and invest our money into areas that lead to more money, not areas that throw money out the window (unless they feed #1).

I know that's a lot. You can't do it all in one step. That's why we've introduced the iterative process and gone back to each domain. We'll do that once more, but first, a refresher on DISC.

Money and DISC

Our DISC style affects the way we think about treasure. It's important to keep the style that resonates with us in mind as we strategize about how to align our treasures. However, we also need to make sure our money feeds all four styles in one way or another because all are necessary.

Drivers are the results-focused people. They are more than happy to spend the entire project budget if it means success. They aren't afraid to go back to school, or earn that certificate or degree they need to earn more. We can learn from the Drivers that risk is acceptable.

The **Influencer** is all about people and fun. You can think of them as your classic impulse buyer. They will easily spend money on the things they love. We can learn from influencers that we need to take a vacation or enjoy that $5 latte.

Steadiness types want consistency and predictability. This shows up either through saving, or letting their significant other take control of the budget. They like to make sure everyone's needs are met. We can learn from Steadiness folks to be generous and collaborate with our spouse on the budget.

Finally, **Conscientious** styles love detail and precision. They budget like none other and probably have spreadsheets with formulas on their computer. They like to make sure everything is accounted for. We can learn from the Conscientious types to make sure we're keeping track of everything, and to put a bit away for the future.

All of us have one of these dominant styles when it comes to money. We can overlay this onto the iterative process and our calling to get even better alignment. Again, none of these types are good or bad. They all have their strengths and weaknesses.

Return of the Iterative Process

As we go through this process, keep ikigai and DISC in mind. Do you tend toward saving or spending? How do you feel about debt and investment? How will you allocate your money to hit every point of ikigai? Once again, lean into the areas that challenge you, and don't spend too long in the areas you feel complacent.

1. Plan

The planning for this process could look like making a daily, weekly, monthly, or annual budget—or a mix. Some styles will be drawn to meticulous accounting, and others want the big picture. Regardless, you need a plan. Make sure all the income and outgo has a place. In other words, take all of your incoming money and assign it to a line item. Include expenses, investments, debts you want to pay off, and of course, fun. If you're new to making a budget, I would recommend beginning with a monthly zero-based budget. If you're subscribed to receive emails from me, you may have already received my basic budget and time sheets. If not, visit InspiredLivingBook.com and you can download them today, along with a number of other resources to help you.

2. Execute

Anyone can make a budget. The real trouble comes with sticking to it. We have to do our best to stay on track with what we've planned—some more than others. Yes, circumstances and unexpected expenses come up, but by and large, we need to follow the plan we've made. So, stick to the budget!

3. Review

At the end of the week or month, balance the budget. Determine what you planned for each line item, and then what you actually spent. You'll find that some line items were unrealistic and needed more money assigned to them—or that you need to cut down on how much you spend in that area. You also may find extra money you didn't know you had, once you start keeping track. This is where many people I coach report feeling like they got a raise, even though their income didn't change.

4. Revise

Remind yourself of your long-term goals when it comes to money, and grade your performance. Determine the areas you need to allocate less money and the areas that need more. Additionally, figure out whether you need to reduce your spending in one area in general. As different circumstances arise through the year, like Christmas, or through circumstances, like a job change, make sure the plan changes accordingly.

5. Repeat

This is where the magic happens. Very few of us will fix our money mindset and performance in a week or month. It comes over time, as we prove to ourselves that we can handle a budget, and we enjoy the benefits from it. Like in the other areas, consistency over time yields the greatest results. As you go through each budget, remember to get 1 percent closer to alignment each time. Dive deep into your underlying beliefs about money so that the changes you experience become lasting.

Specific Strategies

In addition to the iterative process, here are a few strategies that will appeal to different personality styles. Take one or two of them and add them to your iterations. Remember, keep asking yourself, "Why?" as you go, so that your treasure connects with your purpose and calling:

1. Visualize the Future and Mind the Gap

What do you want your life to look like in ten, fifteen, or twenty years? You could even ask yourself the airport question from the previous chapter. What do you want your future self to be able to do, based on their financial situation? Consider your lifestyle, possessions, vacations, retirement, and generosity.

Now, ask yourself why you want those things. For example, maybe you want freedom, the ability to not work the extra job, to say no to overtime, to hang out with your children or aging parents. Your "why" could vary, but make sure it connects with your calling.

Now, identify the gap between where you are now and where you want to be. What do you need to do to close that gap over the long term? How does this vision affect your weekly, monthly, and annual budget?

2. Perform a Long-Term Analysis

This one's perfect for the Conscientious style, though anyone can benefit from this. One time, I worked with a family that was having a hard time sticking to the budget. Part of it was behavioral, but part of it was because they had no clue how much they actually spent on certain things.

So, they reviewed all of their transactions from the past six months. This gave them a baseline of what they spent on each item and identified the problem categories. For one, they were spending excessively on groceries without knowing it. Then, they stuck to a new budget for another six months and determined whether they went over or under on each new line item. This gave them the data they needed for a superb annual budget, and they realized some surprises along the way.

But don't make the mistake of thinking this average amount for any category is the "right" amount to budget for any month . . . We often vary greatly in our spending. For example, our grocery budget in November is usually different from in October. Instead, look at the trends.

3. Identify Plans and Expectations

This family realized they didn't just have problems in one or two areas, though. They identified about twenty areas of spending that were out of control. Some of this was due to a lack of planning, like not actually knowing how much they spend on gas each month. Other problems were behavioral: They spent too much eating out, even when the budget was set. Finally, some were anomalies. For example, a clothing budget might explode during back-to-school season, or a gifts budget during Christmas. Additionally, sometimes life simply throws us curveballs.

This gave them a decision a make: How should they deal with what was unplanned and unexpected? A classic example is car repair. People often say, "I can't plan for the car breaking." Yes, you can. You just can't expect it.

Every single car in the history of cars has required repair. The owners simply didn't always know when it would come up. If a sudden car repair surprises you—what were you expecting? Plan for it by creating a fund for emergencies.

Additionally, the family found that their expectations surrounding groceries didn't meet reality. If you don't actually keep track of what you spend at the grocery store, I can practically guarantee you're spending way more than you'd expect. In this instance, they needed to increase that line item and be slightly more frugal at the store.

4. Sacrifice without Sacrificing

When you take the time to list out everything you're spending money on, it may feel overwhelming. You might feel like you need to sacrifice a ton just to get out of debt or open that retirement account. However, almost everyone has items they spend on that they really don't need. They can give those up, without really feeling like they're giving things up.

Do you really need six streaming services, all billing monthly, or could you survive with one or two? Are you using that gym membership enough to justify the monthly cost? Could you get by eating at home one or two additional nights per week? That last one could save you hundreds of dollars per month, by the way.

5. Don't Quit Your Day Job

This process often shows people that they want a different job. Sometimes they want one more aligned with what they love. Other times, they determine that they really do need to make more money to reach their financial goals. As you walk down the path of getting a new job or starting a new business, don't quit your day job.

Think of it this way: If you quit your job to launch a new business, you're putting yourself in a must-win situation. Failure could mean losing your house or racking up tons of debt. This extra layer of stress will cause you to make poor decisions out of fear or a scarcity mindset. Instead, hold onto what you have now while taking baby steps toward your dream.

6. Don't Sacrifice Too Much on Either End

You won't hear this one much from thought leaders in the financial space. They'll warn you that if you don't bust your back every day for the next few decades, and pinch every penny, that you'll have zero retirement and end up destitute. In other words, you're sacrificing enjoyment of the present for survival in the future.

This isn't reality. I recommend that you don't sacrifice too much on this end. For example, if your dream is to travel during retirement, why not travel a bit now? After all, tomorrow is never guaranteed. You should earmark long-term savings just for travel, but also, work travel into your annual budget.

Some people do sacrifice their retirement years because of shortsightedness today. Others live a completely unenjoyable life just to have a slightly nicer car when they're seventy. I say we should strike a balance. Find ways to live your retirement dreams now. You don't need to have an awful present in order to have a decent future. You can thrive in both; you just need to get clever.

Beyond Compound Interest

Finance gurus love to talk about the power of compound interest, and that's pretty smart. It's important to make sure compound interest works for us in the form of long-term investments, instead of against us in the form of debt. However, there's something even more powerful than compound interest: compound behavior.

I've talked over and over again about the improvements you can make by investing 1 percent each day, or improving at something 1 percent each day. Finances are no different. You can't take hold of good strategies for your treasure unless you become a different kind of person.

You need to slowly align your treasures with your priorities and values while understanding the emotional side. That's why being reasonable instead of rational is important. Beyond this, you really do need to perform the right behaviors consistently for a long time for a positive outcome. This could mean consistently sticking to the budget, consistently maxing out a retirement plan, and/or consistently putting in that little extra at work to gain advancement. Compound behavior will unlock your destiny and allow you to live out your calling. It all comes back to alignment.

Your behaviors come from your attitudes, beliefs, and habits. We want to make sure those align with our "why," our ikigai, our calling and purpose. Leverage your behavior as an investment, a security with a compounding return. This will enable you to develop your influence and impact the world through your time, talents, and yes, treasure.

Chapter Summary

Luke and Lando showed us that we all have a ton of emotions when it comes to finances. When it comes to money, most people get stuck in a cycle of scrounging and then binging, feeling stressed and uneasy the entire time. Instead, we need to find more alignment between our treasure and our calling. We should be reasonable instead of 100 percent rational, given that we are emotional beings who want to thrive both now and later.

When we connect our reason for being with our money, we can determine ways to earn, spend, and save that align with what we love, what the world needs, what we're good at, and what we can get paid to do. When we take the time to understand our personality style, we can see the strengths and weaknesses we bring to our treasure. When we apply both of those to the iterative process, and let our behavior compound over time, we'll find ourselves stewarding our treasure to the fullest. This gives us the most impact through our work, investments, and generosity.

Key Takeaways
- Apply the iterative process to your next monthly budget.
- Determine which specific strategies you'll implement in the next month too.
- Decide exactly how much you'll balance between thriving now and thriving in your retirement years according to your loves.

The Process: How to Complete the Puzzle and Achieve Your Calling

So far, we've covered how to tease out your individual calling. It comes through investing in yourself, and then others. As you go, you get feedback in terms of results, what others tell you, and how certain activities make you feel. Though you may never be able to fully articulate your calling, it will slowly unravel over time.

Then, we talked about our time, talents, and treasures, and how they relate to your calling. They are the loops and sockets needed to hold everything together. We reviewed plenty of strategies suited to various personality styles, but the biggest themes were iteration and alignment. In the quest to make your time, talents, and treasure line up with your calling, you must experiment over and over while making small tweaks.

Now, this is where the rubber meets the road. We're going to look at how to take what we've learned so far and implement it into our lives. This is akin to assembling a puzzle, putting the pieces together so that it paints the picture of our calling and impact. The best way to start this journey is through visualizing the future and reverse engineering from there.

So, let's revisit the airport story. We touched on this during chapter 6. Let's say that in five years, your flight gets delayed and you're stuck at the airport for a few hours. You head into a café and run into a friend whom you haven't seen in five years. They ask you how life is going for you, and you say, "Amazing!"

They ask you why, and you say, "Well, it's because . . ."

What comes after "because"? What happened in your career? Your relationships? Your finances, health, spiritual life, and so on? What are you doing that makes your life so amazing five years from now? Determine the things you're regularly doing and the things that you're not doing.

This gives you the picture on the box. When you assemble a puzzle, you use the box as a reference to put the pieces together. You might have a blue sky up top, a house on the side, and a patch of green grass on the other side. Now you have a general idea of where the pieces go. It also gives you constraints. You begin to understand the pieces that don't belong in your puzzle at all. Nothing illustrates these concepts better than the story of Mark.

Mark is a pseudonym for a real client I had in my coaching business. When we met, he explained that his wife has health issues. He needs to help take care of her during the week since he's the primary caregiver. It takes time in his schedule.

Mark also wanted to grow his marketing business. He's superb at it, and he thought it could help him make money to take care of his wife. So, his challenge was to build a life that let him take care of his wife and excel at his career. We worked out where he wanted to be in five years, and why his life would be so amazing in that airport café, and we started from there. He wanted a business that covered all his needs and wants while freeing up around twenty hours every week for his wife. This gave us the rough outline of the puzzle.

From there, Mark needed to work on the rest of the edges before filling in the middle of the puzzle. After this, he'd need to finalize the puzzle by putting in the last piece. By the end of this process, he'd be in a place where he knew he'd be living out his calling and impacting the world around him. We'll follow the same blueprint to make these principles practical in our own journey.

We'll break down the process of completing the puzzle into the following three chapters:

- Chapter 8: Work the Edges
- Chapter 9: Fill in the Middle
- Chapter 10: The Last Piece to Live Out Your Calling

Chapter 8:

Work the Edges

• • • • • • • • • • •

Not everyone makes it this far, so if you're still here, take a moment to pat yourself on the back. Now, hopefully, you've performed all the steps along the way rather than just speeding through. We have to put these concepts into action if we want real change in our life. So, if you haven't yet, go back and actually do the exercises I outlined in the previous chapters. I promise you, it will pay off in your life. Now, without further ado . . .

Getting this far shows commitment to discovering and living out your unique calling. This part of the book was designed to give you the practical action steps you need to implement what we've learned so far.

So far, we've talked about how to discover your calling. The first step in this process is investing in yourself. If you don't invest in yourself, you won't have anything worthwhile to give others. You'll find your impact in the world diminishing because of that. Only after you consistently invest your own time and money into your health and development can you turn around and invest in others. The currency of investing in others is primarily your time.

This leads to a wider influence over the people around you and the people you lead. As you focus on making a difference, wherever you're at, your unique calling comes into clear focus. It will be reaffirmed by the results you get and the feedback people share with you—not to mention the passion you feel. This will give you an impact in the world—in other words, a useful calling that helps you and others.

Then, we zoomed in on the pieces of the puzzle, or tools we use to live our callings out. The first was our time, arguably the most vital currency we have. Then, we discussed our unique talents and how to hone them. Finally, we talked about our treasure, using money as a tool to leverage impact in the world for our calling.

Now, we need to put it all together. It's one thing to have all the pieces of the puzzle. Now, we need a process to assemble the puzzle. How do we assemble a puzzle? You'll probably find that the first step is to work the edges.

Opening up a one thousand-piece puzzle looks daunting at first, but if you look at the pieces, you'll notice that a small proportion of them have straight edges instead of curves. This means they have to go on the edge of the puzzle someplace. This makes it much easier to find matching pieces and the appropriate place for each piece to go. You might even get lucky and find a piece with two straight edges, representing a corner. That can go only one of four places.

Building out the edges of the puzzle gives you the zone to work in. It also sets the parameters; no piece will go outside this border. Plus, you can already see the outline of the big picture.

That's the first step. In terms of Inspired Living, what does it mean to work the edges?

Tim Knifton: Determining What You Want Out of Life

Tim Knifton is a serial entrepreneur who loves to start and grow new businesses. When he isn't working on a business in the marketing space or selling a business in the IT space, he works on building houses on his rental properties.

If you're searching for deep fulfillment in your personal and professional life, it takes more than just "doing what you love." Sure, that's important, but there's more that goes into it. In my own life and working with others, I've discovered many truths that shed some light on the age-old question: "What do I want out of life?" We could write libraries' worth on this subject, but for now, let's cover just three things you ought to consider.

First, you have to realize that anything you pursue is ten to twenty years out from showing tangible results over the long term. We live in an age of instant gratification and endless opportunities, which isn't negative by itself. However, we forget that any pursuit or passion takes years of experimentation and development. That's okay! That's why you want to enjoy the journey and not hyperfocus on the destination.

Second, as you determine your personal and professional goals, remember to align them with your own beliefs. This may seem obvious, but I see so many people setting goals that are "practical" but don't make sense for them. Don't fall for it! Aligning your goals with your beliefs is key to feeling satisfied in your life.

Finally, as you put your puzzle together, you may find certain pieces no longer fit, even if they're exciting and possibly lucrative opportunities. Over the years, I had to learn to say no more often than I said yes. As tempting as it feels to try to fit everything in, resist that temptation. To stay true to your goals and beliefs, you'll often have to remove those unfitting puzzle pieces. Above all, learn to say, "No." That's how you stay focused and make progress toward *your* goals, not someone else's.

Mark Determined His Edges

> Once you determine your family and business goals, you'll find that many puzzle pieces no longer fit in your puzzle.
>
> —Tim Knifton

I introduced you to Mark during the introduction to part 3. He felt torn between wanting a business that could support his family and taking care of his wife, who needed at-home care for a significant chunk of the week. To Mark, this felt constraining. When he was at work, he'd feel guilty that he wasn't with his wife. When he spent time taking care of his wife, he felt guilty that he wasn't earning money.

I suggested a new way of looking at it. These constraints weren't handcuffs; they were the edges of his puzzle. He wanted to spend sixty hours a week working in his business, and twenty taking care of his wife. However, that was impossible. After all, he needed to eat, sleep, and take care of his own health.

We looked a little deeper at the assumptions he was making. He figured that to succeed in his marketing business, he needed to spend sixty hours every week working on it. But was that true? Working a certain number of hours each week doesn't arbitrarily guarantee a certain amount of income. In addition, how much income did Mark and his family really need?

We got answers to those questions. Instead of thinking, "How can I survive working sixty hours and taking care of my wife for twenty?" the question became "How can I make an income that takes care of our needs and wants in twenty to thirty hours per week?" This way, when he's at work, he wouldn't feel guilty about being apart from his wife since he would easily be able to spend twenty hours a week taking care of her without burning out.

With this, the picture became more clear. We started to have the edges of the puzzle. Now, we needed to find work for him that made him feel aligned, all the way to the core. Sure, we didn't have every piece of the puzzle figured out yet (like how physical health and his spiritual life came into play), but we had enough edge pieces to see the big picture. That's where it starts. After all . . .

You Don't Need to Know All the Answers

In a real-life puzzle, you might have to put 100 percent of the edge pieces together before moving on to the middle pieces. Not so in real life. You might find yourself missing a piece or two before you move on, and that's okay. You don't need to have all the answers to your personal passions or even the constraints you need to operate in. Remember how we said it's an iterative process that reveals itself over time? Mark had two pieces of his puzzle, and that was enough for him to get going.

Likewise, you can get started on the inside of your puzzle before everything is done. In fact, I've never met anyone who claims to have every piece figured out—unless they were trying to sell me something.

So, focus on the basic structure. The puzzle itself is fluid. It changes over time. The important part is to build out enough of the edges that you can see the big picture, and then keep that end state in mind. For example, Mark could have gotten into a place in his business where he only needed to work fifteen hours per week to make the income he needed. Then he'd have to figure out how to spend the additional time. Or, maybe his wife could get to a place of health where he didn't need to spend as many hours taking care of her. He could choose to reinvest that time elsewhere too. The edges of your puzzle will shift slowly, but the big picture will remain the same and reveal itself over time.

Lastly, don't compare your puzzle to someone else's! This is your puzzle. Mark fell into this trap. He looked around and saw other professionals working sixty hours a week to be "successful," and he assumed the same applied to him. However, it turned out he had certain skills that, when properly marketed and applied, helped him pay all his bills and take care of his wife—regardless of what other people were doing. Today, he lives debt-free and runs a profitable business that allows him to be with his wife for five to eight hours every day.

These Five Questions Will Help You Work the Edges

Let's get practical. How do we work the edges? What if we don't really know about the time, treasure, and talents at our disposal? That's where these five questions come into play. At this point, we have at least a foggy idea of our calling. We know the general direction we want to move toward. Now we need to fill out the frame of what our life will really look like; the things we need to do every day and week to get to our vision.

I have five questions that I ask clients to help them understand what they need to do. Your consistent actions will shape your destiny. To live out your calling, you need to change your everyday life around. So, these questions all have to do with your tasks and actions. The more clearly and robustly you answer them, the more edge pieces you will have. Again, it's perfectly fine to not know the answer to a particular question, but do your best.

Question 1

What are you doing now, that you love, that you should be doing?

In other words, these are the actions you currently take, that you love to do, that build you toward that future. If you want to become a pilot, then ideally, the action of flying a plane falls in this category. So might performing flight instruction. This question might seem like a no-brainer, but it's important to step back and realize that you are most likely doing things right now that build toward your ideal future. Keep track of them so that you don't stop doing them.

What do you do with these kinds of tasks? You continue doing them, and you enjoy them. They are like the dessert to your day. If you want to become an author, you might spend a great deal of time each day outlining and researching, and a small portion actually doing the writing, which you enjoy most. So, when it comes around, savor it.

Question 2

What are you doing now, that you hate, that you should be doing?

In other words, what are the distasteful tasks that you ought to perform to build you toward that future. You need to write these out too. For me, it's actually writing. I enjoy hosting podcasts and talking to people, so those would fall in the first category. However, writing builds my future too, and I know I should do it. That doesn't mean I have to like it, though!

There's an additional wrinkle to this: many people say they do these, but when you actually run the numbers, they really don't.

Let me put it another way. We all have stuff we should be doing, but we're not actually doing it, because we hate to do it. Sometimes, we lie to ourselves and say we're doing it more often than we actually are. Even though these tasks are often the direct path for us to meet our goals.

> Are you doing what you say you're doing?
>
> —Ron Mills

Think of someone who wants to grow their brand. They could benefit from appearing on podcasts by leaders in their industry three times a week or more. But they hate speaking on podcasts. So perhaps they only do it once a week, or none at all. Or, take going to church on Sunday. Many people call themselves church-goers, but when you actually run the numbers, they only go to church about once every month.

So, run the numbers. Determine whether you're actually doing this task that you hate. Then, realize that it's the direct path to your calling. Many people want to become marketers or consultants, but they hate cold calling or pitching their work to people, and so they avoid it. Others want to become authors, but they despise sitting down and writing. Still, those tasks will directly lead them to living out their calling.

For these tasks, we need to keep doing them. And we also need to consider modifying the tasks to make them easier or more enjoyable for us. More on that under Question 4.

Question 3

What are you not doing, that you love, that you should be doing?

This is a fun one. In other words, you need to ask yourself whether there's something you like doing that could actually help you toward your goal! Say you want to lose twenty pounds. Perhaps you hate running on a treadmill, but you love running on trails in the woods. Identify that fact, and build it into your schedule.

You might ask, "If I love it and I should be doing it, wouldn't I already be doing it? Why is this even a category?" The answer has to do with the edges of the puzzle. You and I are not doing everything we should be doing, even things we enjoy, because time is finite. We tend to fill our time with activities that don't build our future at all, like social media and Netflix. So, even enjoyable tasks that help us fall by the wayside.

To remedy this, keep track of your time. I mentioned a couple of exercises for that back in chapter 5. Determine your list of activities you need to do that you actually love, and build time into your schedule for them. Then, for these tasks, start them and enjoy them while you perform them.

Question 4

What are you not doing, that you hate, that you should be doing?

This is probably the toughest question to answer. Sometimes, it has guilt and shame attached to it. Here, we realize that there are often plenty of tasks that could help us get to our desired future, but we don't like doing them. So we don't. The would-be author discovers they aren't plugging one to two thousand words into their keyboard each day. The would-be entrepreneur comes to terms with the fact that they don't have a solid business plan or the formal education they need.

> Instead of just doing things I'm really strong at, I look for things that balance me out and develop my whole person.
> —Tim Knifton

There's bad news and good news. The bad news is, much like the tasks from Question 2 (tasks you are doing, that you hate, that you should be doing), *you still need to do these tasks.* But you also need to surmount the initial obstacle of getting started and building the habit from scratch. All the while, you hate doing the task in the first place.

The good news is, you can modify the task to make it easier or more enjoyable. There are two main paths for modification:

1. Get Outside Help

Say your business needs a weekly blog to drum up some traffic to your website, but you hate writing. Instead of avoiding the task and reaping the consequences, consider outsourcing the blog to someone else. This way, the task still gets done. You just trade your money for someone else's time and energy. You buy your enjoyment back. Perhaps part of your calling involves getting into better shape, but you hate planning and executing workouts. To make it easier, hire a fitness coach who tells you exactly what to do. The list goes on.

Additionally, you don't need to always solve the problem with money. You could come to an agreement with someone else. Say you have a fantastic idea for a product that you know people will love, but you aren't the best at sales and marketing. Consider partnering with someone who is, and split the profits from your amazing idea. For example, I mentioned before that I hate writing. So, I got outside help to make the process easier for me. That way, I got to focus on my strengths.

2. Find a Different Way toward the Same Result

Another way to modify a task is to consider the end result you desire. Sometimes, the task you hate isn't the only way to get what you need. For example, if your business needs a blog, but you hate blogging, take a step back. What it really requires, rather than a blog, is a platform for attracting an audience and building brand authority. That certainly could be accomplished through a blog, but it could also be accomplished through a podcast, or through social media communities. Take whichever of those tasks you enjoy the most, and do that instead.

Personally, I love podcasting far more than blogging or authoring. At the time of this writing, I have a podcast called *Inspired*

Stewardship with over 1,300 episodes. After years of trying so many things, I found a method of communication that gives me the results I want.

The idea is to figure out *why* you're doing the task you hate. When you discover the fundamental reason beneath that task, alternate paths may appear. Don't assume you already know exactly what tasks are needed. Instead, determine the big picture you're moving toward, and select the most enjoyable tasks to get there.

Still, the time will come when you need to start or continue doing a task you hate because it builds the future you want. Such is life. I wish that living out our calling felt enjoyable and fulfilling every moment of every day, but it simply doesn't. We need to develop discipline and habits to help us get through tasks we don't enjoy, when we know we need to do them. The first step there is complete self-honesty.

Let's sum up the first four questions. I made a handy diagram that will show you each question and how to respond:

Task/Actions	Doing?	Not Doing?
Love?	Enjoy and Continue	Start and Enjoy
Hate?	Modify and Continue	Modify and Start

You can use these boxes as a kind of flow chart. Make sure you write out the tasks that go into each box and make the decision to respond accordingly. We can't just talk about our calling; we have to live it out. We've talked about how the habits we form and the tasks we do consistently will enable us to live out our calling. There's no other way.

When we answer the first four questions (and live them out), we'll find ourselves doing everything we should be doing to get to our calling. We'll have a much better idea of our constraints too! That's because if we really fill our schedule with actions that will help us, whether we enjoy them or not, we'll find ourselves running up against the barriers of our time, treasure, and talents pretty quickly. That's when Question 5 comes into play . . .

Question 5
What are you doing that you shouldn't be doing?

Previously, every question ended in "should be doing." But that's only one side of the story. You and I also engage in plenty of activities that we shouldn't be doing. They aren't necessarily evil (though some might be), but they certainly won't get us to that five-year plan we made in the airport exercise.

Think of it this way: Most people have a to-do list that's way too long, full of stuff they know they will probably never get around to. But do you have a "not to do" list? An assortment of activities you ban yourself from doing? The most successful people do.

This is where sacrifice comes into play. Inspired Living, a life of living out our calling and impacting the world, requires great sacrifice. Otherwise, everyone would do it. However, some people count up the costs and then walk away. Still, some people realign their lives, starting and continuing what they should be doing, and stopping what they shouldn't.

What do we do with these tasks? Well, the answer might be obvious: We stop. We let go of that task, and learn to live without it. This is often the most difficult part of the entire process. For Mark, he had to stop working sixty hours a week and start working thirty. It meant he couldn't use work as a drug, and it also meant he would make less money.

That's often what it comes down to, in Question 5. Fear and scarcity. It certainly came up in my story. When I decided I wanted to leave the corporate world and pursue what I do now, my biggest fear involved money. So, my wife and I came together and figured out a plan. We knew that I was going to stop my old job, but we also knew the time wasn't quite right. We needed to take a year and tighten our belts to save up.

I knew that if I started this business, I would run away from it the moment I thought I couldn't provide for my family. So, we saved ourselves a cushion of money to make the transition easier. We had to stop many things that year. We had fewer vacations, fewer times eating out, fewer luxuries in general. It was tough. But if we wanted to save money, then "going to Disneyland" fell into the "shouldn't be doing" category.

It was made easier because we understood our *why*. We had an idea of the big picture. Saving that cushion of money that year gave us the edges of our puzzle. We knew the space we had to work within. After a year, I had the leeway I needed to leave my job and start what I do now. It was kind of like the runway before taking off.

To get there, I kept my actions focused on where I was going. I answered all five questions. I had to continue and enjoy being a father and a husband. I also had to start and enjoy a podcast and begin networking with people to learn as much as I could before I started. I had to continue and hate my corporate job for an entire year, because it was what I should be doing to save that money. I had to start (and not particularly enjoy) building a website and writing. Lastly, I had to stop spending my money on a multitude of things I was used to. It was a sacrifice to live below our means for a long time; it took vision and agreement for us to get there.

However, by the end of it? I was doing everything I should be, and not doing anything I shouldn't. And that led directly to the goal. It wouldn't have been possible, however, unless I began by answering those questions and working the edges.

Pour Out the Pieces

> I don't just do something that I have a lot of passion for and that I'm really great at. It's really about doing the things that help me reach my goals.
> —Tim Knifton

When you buy a new puzzle, you get a nice box with an image of the completed work. You unwrap the plastic, open it up, breathe in that new puzzle smell, and pour all the pieces onto the table. That's the next step for you.

It will be messy. It will feel overwhelming at first. Beginning to live out your calling and impacting the world will feel that way. However, you have all the tools you need to get started. You have an idea of your calling and what you want your life to look like in five years. That's what part 1 of the book and the airport exercise were about, respectively. You also have an idea of how your time, treasure, and talents fit into all this. That was part 2. You know the way you need to structure your day, the skills you need to develop and gain, and the way to steward your finances to get you there.

Next comes lining up the edge pieces through the questions above, and then starting on the puzzle. But that's only after you pour out the pieces. Once you pour them onto the table, it's much harder to put them all back in the box and forget about your dream until later. Make the intentional decision that you will move toward your vision. We've talked about a great deal of theory and concepts so far; now it's time to act. Don't read on to the next chapter until you pour out the puzzle pieces, whatever that looks like.

It could mean writing out your five-year plan and getting your spouse or best friend to read it. Maybe you need to create a contract or agreement with yourself that you sign to keep yourself on track. Perhaps you need to call someone you trust and ask them to keep you accountable. Do whatever it takes to wake up *different* tomorrow morning, ready to take the first steps toward your plan.

Pour out the pieces, and get going.

Chapter Summary

Putting together a puzzle can feel daunting at first. Whenever I do it, I mitigate this by working the edges first. This means getting the border pieces all lined up and in their proper places before moving on with the rest of the pieces. This gives me constraints, an idea of the bigger picture, and a feeling of progress.

The same goes in your journey toward your calling. You need to determine the parameters around your picture so that you know where to build. The best way to do this is by determining what you should be doing, and what you shouldn't be doing. When you should be doing a task that you don't enjoy, find a way to modify it. When you should be doing something you enjoy, savor it. Lastly, when you identify something you shouldn't be doing, get ready to sacrifice. This is what it takes to begin living out your calling.

Key Takeaways

- If you haven't yet, perform the airport exercise. Get specific on what you want your life to look like in five years, and why it's so amazing compared to the previous periods.

- Answer the first four questions to determine what you should be doing to get there, and find ways to modify as many tasks as you can that you don't enjoy.
- Honestly and vulnerably, determine the things you need to stop doing, whether they are a distraction or even an addiction.

Chapter 9:

Fill in the Middle

. . . .

The pilot is cleared for takeoff. They begin accelerating down the runway at breakneck speeds. At just the right moment, lift-off occurs. The pilot cautiously scans all the instrumentation to make sure nothing will go wrong, knowing that most problems occur quickly after takeoff. After some elevation, they retract the landing gear. The airplane begins climbing up, up, and over the clouds. Then, the pilot does next to nothing for several hours besides ensuring the course is held.

The exciting events happen at the very beginning and very end of the plane ride. The middle? Not so much. Once you get to altitude, the plane practically flies itself to the destination. However, the pilot still must remain concentrated. They need to make sure everything that needs to be happening, happens. They must continue to monitor the minute details of the situation. Here, it becomes all about consistency.

The same is true in our journey to Inspired Living and in our puzzle assembly. By this point, we've worked the edges. We may not have every piece of the border in place, but we certainly have enough to go on. The big picture has started to come into place.

However, the edge pieces only make up a tiny fraction of the work to be done.

This happens in our journey. We begin planning to change jobs to something more aligned with our calling in our career, or we set out on a diet. At first, during the planning and first steps, everything feels exciting. We can see the big picture, and we can practically taste the result. But after a little while, it starts to get increasingly difficult. It's not necessarily fun to prepare a résumé and apply to fifty jobs in a row, making time for interviews and getting rejected or ignored. Neither is it fun to eat the same food day in and day out, and avoid that treat you've been craving.

We've entered the long middle. It's very simple, comparatively speaking, for the pilot to fly the plane for 95 percent of the time. Takeoff and landing are the parts that require skill. However, remaining concentrated and consistent? That's tough.

In order to fill in our middle, we need to put small pieces into place over a long period of time, keeping the big picture in mind while working in the trenches. It's simple, but it isn't easy. It ultimately boils down to the two main types of tasks we covered in the last chapter: things we should be doing, and things we shouldn't.

We should do everything that builds our future and gets us closer to living out our calling and impacting the world. We should stop doing everything that gets in the way. It's a simple equation. But it's the hardest part of the entire journey.

Wade Galt: Work, Rest, and Impact

Wade Galt helps entrepreneurs and professionals create a "3-Day Weekend" lifestyle, one where people thrive sustainably in their rhythm of work and rest and perform work they actually enjoy.

It's easy to get so caught up in the professional grind that you forget about your life outside of work. If you're not seeing the results you want, it's probably because you're lost in the hustle and aren't giving yourself a fruitful personal life. I'm a big believer that we can design a life with ample downtime while getting done what we need to.

For starters, don't work too much. You know the folks who plan the wedding but never bother to plan the marriage? That's what happens when you devote all of your time and energy toward one pursuit, but then you forget about your personal life. Working harder does not necessarily guarantee better results—it's like you started cutting your lawn with scissors instead of a lawnmower. Working harder is not always better, especially in today's age. Make sure you enrich your personal life just as much (or more!) as your professional life. You've got to plan the marriage too.

You also have to remember that progress comes from taking action every day, however small. It reminds me of the book *The Power of Less* by Leo Babauta, which shows us how small, daily wins are the key to consistent growth. So if you're learning how to swim, practice for just five minutes every day. Soon, those five minutes will become ten, then fifteen, and so on. That's how you build a habit of growth.

Finally, it's crucial to be obsessively accountable to your process. What do I mean? Maybe something in your process stopped working two weeks ago, but you never caught it. So you're probably slowing yourself down without even knowing it. That's why you need to routinely and meticulously refine your process, dropping whatever's decreasing your efficiency. By having this awareness, you'll maintain your momentum, see results more often, and most importantly, be able to design your life on your terms. Don't settle for a two-day weekend if you don't have to!

There's a Difference between Simple and Easy

> There's this belief that there's a linear connection between effort and results, yet we know that's not the case.
> —**Wade Galt**

"Just diet and exercise, and you'll lose weight."

"Want to write a book? Just sit down and write one thousand words each day."

"Just apply to jobs until you get hired if you want a new career."

"Want to live out your calling? Just start doing what you should be doing, and stop doing what you shouldn't."

Simple enough, right? And the truth is, it is very simple. If I had to ask you to list out five things you should be doing that help you and five things you should stop doing, you could probably tell me.

But it isn't easy. In fact, it's so difficult that it separates the successful from the unsuccessful. Take a look at the most extraordinarily successful people who definitely live out their calling from day to day, and they'll all have one thing in common: They do what they should do. Consistently and excellently. They also avoid doing what they shouldn't do. Consistently.

By the way, success doesn't mean money and fame. Take your favorite teacher in school, for instance, one who impacted you more than anyone else. They showed up, day in and day out, and they probably aren't a millionaire at the moment. Or, think of this way: Have you ever been to the funeral of a truly great person? Not one who was necessarily rich or famous, but one who everyone had a deep sense of gratitude for. This person did what they should have done, year in and year out. This gave them a place of honor in everyone's memory. Regardless of their wealth or fame, they impacted the world through their calling.

To be like them, you have to fill in the middle. You have to stop doing what you shouldn't do, the habits, addictions, and distractions that hold you back from your calling. At the same time, you have to do the things that will build your future, regardless of whether you find them enjoyable.

So, How Do We Fill in the Middle?

There are multiple practical tools, tactics, and people that can help you fill in the middle. This is a long process requiring utmost consistency. You're like the pilot watching the plane fly itself to the destination, keeping a monitor on everything that needs to be done to ensure it. However, most of the process may just feel like waiting. And temptation. And distractions. And the desire to slack off on things you should be doing but don't enjoy. So, fill your tool belt up with everything you can to ensure you progress toward the end vision.

1. Involve Others to Hold You Accountable

Part of the reason every pilot has a copilot is to make sure someone can fly the plane if the pilot gets sick or has a heart attack. However, they also ensure the pilot does their job. Every human feels the temptation to cut corners when nobody's looking, especially if it means getting things done faster, or serving their "right now" at the expense of their calling.

So, get yourself a copilot. It could be a member of your family, a friend, a like-minded accountability partner, a group, a mentor, or a coach. If you need accountability to stop doing something that's hard to stop, like an addiction, you might need to bring in a professional.

This person is not a "yes" person. They don't go along with everything you say. They don't enable you. When the worst of you comes to the surface, they call it out as they see it. They ask you whether you did what you should have done, especially the tasks you don't enjoy. And they asked if you did what you shouldn't have done, especially the actions that will hold you up the most.

However, this person is also not a "Debbie Downer." They encourage you rather than tear you down. They remind you that you can meet your goals, that it isn't impossible for you. When you have a failure or setback, you find them right by your side, helping you get back up. Strike the balance between these two ends of the spectrum, and you'll find a fantastic accountability person.

Many of the people I coach use their spouse as the person for accountability. Nobody is more personally invested in your calling than they are. I remember one client told me how he sat down with his wife and showed her all of his plans for his side business, one aligned with his true calling. His wife gave feedback on different phases of his plan and ensured he stayed on track. She especially ensured that he didn't overinvest in his side hustle while working his traditional job so that everything got done in the right order.

> Happy is the man who finds a true friend, and far happier is he who finds that true friend in his wife.
> —Franz Schubert

When you have your accountability person, give them a simple job. Tell them to stop you from doing things you shouldn't be doing and to keep you doing what you should. They can handle most of the tasks with a simple text or phone conversation.

Say you want to stop binging Netflix because it's distracting you from living out your calling. Nothing is wrong with enjoying TV or movies, by the way, but doing it most days of the week for several hours at a time can keep you away from impacting the world. So, text your accountability person about your Netflix habits. Keep them in the loop. The act of telling someone else about what you're doing automatically motivates you toward better things, so long as you remain honest with them.

Speaking of kicking a Netflix habit . . .

2. Create Friction (or Smoothness)

Set up your life to make it more difficult to do things you shouldn't, and easier to do things you should. Let's run with the Netflix example. If you want to binge-watch less, create friction around the act of binge-watching. Make it harder to perform. For example, you could log out of Netflix every time you finish using it.

The act of logging into Netflix at the beginning of your session doesn't sound like it would stop you, but it might. Even if I know the password to my account, taking the time to clumsily punch it in with a remote is a hassle. I hate hassle. It takes an additional minute or two just to get started. Sometimes, I'll open up Netflix, remember that I need to log in, see the friction, then decide it isn't worth it. You can apply the concept of creating friction to everything you shouldn't be doing.

If you need to stop eating a certain comfort food, stop keeping it in the house. The same goes for alcohol if you have too much of it regularly. If you need to stop wasting time on social media, remove the apps from your phone. If you really need to get some writing or other work done on the computer, maybe give your phone to your spouse and tell them to keep it from you until you're done.

The next step? Make it as easy as possible to do what you should. If you need to get up early, crank up your alarm and put it outside your room so you have to physically get up to turn it off. If you need to go on a morning run, put all your jogging gear right next to your bed—or even sleep in your running shorts. If you're working on writing a book, make the manuscript your internet browser's home page instead of your email inbox or a social media account. Need to record a podcast? Hire an editor and create an agreement where you pay them every week, regardless of whether you have recorded an episode. You had better believe that when you do that, you'll make sure to get the recording done!

We know that it's simple, but not easy, to do the right things and avoid the wrong things. So, stack the odds in your favor in whatever ways you can. Eventually, it will get easier due to the nature of habits.

3. Revisit Habits

We talked about habits during chapter 5, and here's a fantastic time to revisit them. Make the tasks you need to perform into habits so they go from "This is what I need to do" to "This is just what I do." The less time your brain has to think about it, and potentially throw out an excuse or distraction, the better.

Remember the habit loop: cue, routine, reward, repeat. This loop can benefit us or destroy us. For some, the cue might be a stressful event in our day, and the habit is to hop onto Amazon and see whether we can buy anything. The reward comes in the form of that tiny dopamine hit we get from hitting "buy." If nothing changes in our lives, this loop will repeat ad infinitum.

Thankfully, we can hack it. For one, we get to decide our routines. That's why I recommend doing the same thing every morning and evening if it suits your personality. I also recommend a routine for beginning and ending your workday, to get into and out of the work mode. We already know most of what we need to do. What remains is to wire them into our daily lives.

Additionally, we can experiment with rewards. The rewards for buying that shiny object or eating that cheeseburger are powerful, but highly temporary. You can give yourself better rewards for the right actions. For example, you could treat yourself to your favorite meal or restaurant when you successfully record four podcasts in a month. Or, you could give yourself a week off work if you complete that book.

Finally, make sure you identify and isolate the cues for your bad habits. Perhaps you find yourself drinking too much when you go out to eat with a certain group of friends. While the problem behavior might be the drinking, it's much easier to manipulate the cue long before you even get into that situation. This could look like finding a new group of friends, ones who encourage you in a better way. Or, it could mean that when you go out with them, you go to a place that doesn't serve alcohol. Whatever you need to stop doing, take a step back and figure out the trigger.

4. Talk to a Pro

Not every bad habit can be overcome by hacking the habit loop on your own. Some habits can feel next to impossible to break. We've entered the territory of addictions. Please don't take my advice about friction and habit hacking as the cure-all for any addiction in your life. Some issues we have require extra firepower beyond the normal tools at our disposal. Someone needs to go under the surface and check out our internal plumbing.

Imagine you had a problem with the plumbing in your house. No matter what you do, all the faucets spew out icky brown water instead of something you could actually drink. Chances are high that you don't understand how plumbing works. If you try to go under your sink or into the pipes beyond your walls, you could potentially make everything worse. In this instance, you would call a professional who knows how to deal with this kind of problem. They've seen this type of issue a thousand times and can easily work toward a solution.

The same goes for talking to a professional. There's no shame in bringing in an expert trained in dealing with problems like yours, just like there's no shame in calling a plumber when your sink isn't working properly. If you're struggling with an addiction, the best thing you can do is stop trying to face it on your own. Get a counselor, get into a group, and/or talk to a specialist.

5. Use Technology Tools

> Our most important currency, our time,
> we don't even put on the negotiation table.
> **—Wade Galt**

Next, implement technology to help you do what you should and avoid what you shouldn't. Oftentimes, people bemoan the fact that we live in such a technological age because it can create so many distractions for us. While that may be the case, technology can still fulfill its intended purpose of making life easier for us—we just need to know how to use it.

Take plant lighting timers, for instance. Some plants want light and heat only at certain times of the day, so some stores sell special power outlets that you can program for this purpose. I have a friend who bought one, and he uses it for his television. He programmed it so that it only powers the TV during certain hours of the day, and he nestled the power outlet so far back into his entertainment center that it would cause a huge hassle to override.

There are also a thousand technological tools that can help us on our smartphones and laptops. I currently use Daywise, an app that batches all my notifications and only sends them to me at specified times of the day. When I need to write, record a podcast, or coach someone, the last thing I need is a bunch of emails and texts to distract me. Getting them all at the beginning and end of the workday helps me get through them faster and be more productive throughout the day.

There are apps that remind you to hydrate or walk around, desks that make you stand up at certain times, apps that block or unsubscribe you from email lists, timers that help you get more done in the same amount of time . . . The applications here are endless (pun intended). Think of ways you can leverage technology to your advantage instead of letting it distract you. Remember, the tech itself is a neutral entity, incapable of helping or hindering you on its own. You get to decide how it relates to you on your journey.

Here Are More Specific Strategies and Advice

The following strategies are specific applications of the principles above, wired toward specific personality types. Remember, not every kind of person resonates with the same tools, so I want to offer a variety. Try each of these and see whether any of them help you, and if they do, go with them.

1. Match Systems to Your Personality

Remember the DISC? It's a fantastic way to determine what will help you best when it comes to overcoming obstacles and getting productive with what you should be doing. For example, it could show you the main distractions you might face. Drivers might get distracted by the big picture, or an amazing new idea, while skipping steps and missing important details. Influencer types might get distracted by people or workplace politics. Steadiness types might feel rushed and freeze up, or get distracted by an argument they had earlier that day. Conscientious people might hyper fixate on the details of a procedure, or the layout of their office space, while others pass them by.

That's the value of understanding yourself. When you do this, you can begin to find the right mentors and tools for you. As I said previously, most productivity hacks are written for the "C" type of person. If that's not you, then you might struggle to implement them and then wonder what's wrong. Nothing's wrong; you simply need to find the right system for your personality type. Keep iterating until you find the fit for you.

2. Iterate

When you fill out a puzzle, you often try a few different pieces in each slot before finding the right fit. You might think that something works where it is, only to go back later and change your mind. The same is true for this process. That's why I keep returning to the iterative process of plan, execute, review, revise, and repeat. Some personalities will treat this like a science experiment, changing just one variable at a time and meticulously recording the results. Others will make more drastic changes and go by their gut feeling. There isn't a wrong answer to this.

The only way to lose at this game is to not play. Some of your puzzle pieces, you'll find, don't actually belong in your picture at all. Others will for a time, then need to get reassembled elsewhere down the line. Unlike a physical puzzle, this one will feel more fluid to your experience. Over time, you'll learn from what doesn't work and from what does. The beautiful part is, every move you make gives you some feedback. Over time, the picture begins to get more clear, and you'll intuitively feel when you're on the right track.

3. Implement Planned Disruption

> Make sure you have time to enjoy your family, your friends, your hobbies, your freedom, and your life outside of work.
> —Wade Galt

This tactic helps those who get bogged down in the details, get distracted by people, or feel tempted to stress out and worry. We need to disrupt ourselves periodically to get back on the right track. When I was a science teacher, I would only teach each period for about fifty minutes. It turns out, that's about as long as a person can focus on one task before needing a break. So, once per hour, the students would get up, walk to a different part of the campus, and switch subjects.

Implement the same in your day-to-day. Give yourself an hour at a time, then take a lap around your house or to the end of the street. What you actually do during the planned disruption can vary, but I recommend a different category of action. So, if you did something physical, break it up with a mental task like a quick crossword puzzle. If you did something that required a ton of focus, do something creative like taking a couple of artsy photos around your neighborhood.

This helps us reenergize for the next hour, but it also knocks us out of bad habits. If we find ourselves scrolling endlessly on social media when that timer goes off, the disruption allows us to break the cycle and make a different choice after the break. It gives you a moment to reassess what you're doing and whether it helps you toward your future goals.

4. Plan for Things to Go Sideways

Most of what we've discussed assumes the best-case scenario. However, we know that life is filled with distractions, hazards, and tragedies. As a Christian, I know that people are not promised easy lives. That's simply not how it's going to go.

So, work this fact into your plans. When you begin a project, give yourself a bit of a buffer at the end to complete it. Why? Because it will likely take longer than you plan for. When things ultimately do go sideways, you have the power to detach from it and not freak out, because you were planning for it. Shift your mentality so that when everything does go perfectly well, you're pleasantly surprised.

Also, take the time now to identify who your biggest cheer-leaders are. You will lean on these folks when life throws you a curveball. Don't wait until something bad happens to develop and maintain these special relationships. Also, determine the inner resources you have to help when life happens. Do you have a strong faith, a good community, an outlet for diffusing stress? If not, develop them now. You'll thank yourself later.

5. Plan for Slow Progress

On a related note, ask yourself this: "Am I okay if it takes me longer than I anticipated?"

Say you want to switch careers, and you plan to save up money for a year, like I did. Are you okay if it takes two or three years? Because it might. Or, say you want to write a book in the next three months. Do you have a fallback plan in case it starts taking longer, or will you start to lose hope and give up?

This relates to the concept of progress over perfect.

(Yes, I said "perfect," instead of "perfection," because guess what? It's a grammatically imperfect way to say it.)

To be frank with you, I'm still not entirely living out my own calling. I'm not some perfect guru, descending from the heavens to show you the way. I'm a regular guy who's figuring it out too. My life looks tremendously more like my calling every year, and my impact has grown too—but I'm still not where I want to be in every area. Progress comes slowly. However, it is progress. The worst thing we can do here is throw up our hands when we feel like progress is too slow and quit.

Do Not Quit. Find the Right Fit.

Yes, you can quit. I can't leap through the pages of this book and force you to start living out your calling and impacting the world. However, I don't need to. The fact that you've made it this far says quite a bit. Too many people give up early, but you didn't. You've been powering through to the end of this book, earnestly seeking how to live an inspired life.

Sometimes, you fail to make progress, or make it slowly, not because you're a failure, or because you can't do it. It more likely means you haven't found the right tool or technique yet. Assembling the middle of the puzzle will become an ongoing process of trying different techniques out, seeing what fits, and chipping away at the big picture. It will take longer than you think, but as you look back month after month, year after year, you'll see progress. You won't be the same person you were when you started.

So, pick up the next piece of the puzzle and find the place for it. Get the right tool, mentor, accountability person, and technique. And continually iterate on the process. Your self-awareness will grow, and the path toward Inspired Living will begin to open up.

I promise you that if you don't quit, you'll start to see the pieces falling into place.

Chapter Summary

While the beginning of the journey comes with excitement and enthusiasm, when we set out on a journey to discover our calling and improve our lives, we eventually settle into the long middle. The edges are defined, and now we see hundreds or thousands of small puzzle pieces to assemble. How do we fill in the middle? We keep doing everything we should, and we stop doing everything we shouldn't.

It's simple, but it's far from easy. It separates the people who come alive and successfully impact the world from those who never make it. So, we need to make it as easy as possible for ourselves. This involves a process of discovering the right people to bring into the journey and the right tools and strategies to implement. It will take longer than we expect, but over time, we'll iterate and iterate until we see the pieces come together.

Key Takeaways

- Identify a few candidates to become your accountability person, and then talk to them about your goals.
- Make it easier to do what you should and harder to do what you shouldn't through habits, friction, professional help, and technology tools.
- As you go, determine which specific strategies benefit your personality type. Whatever you do, don't quit.

Chapter 10:

The Last Piece to Live Out Your Calling

· ·

Remember Peder, from the beginning of the book?

He and his wife have gotten to the point where she no longer has to work extra. In fact, she has the option to go part-time if she wants, though that's a big deal since her job is a big part of her calling. Peder's business has tripled in revenue and profit, and he actually brought on his first hire recently. By the time you read this, they'll most likely have paid off their house. They still meet with me today.

Don't get me wrong, their process had its ups and downs. But they made progress. They iterated, instead of remaining paralyzed. Now, they almost have all the tools in place to begin assembling a new puzzle.

After a long process of working the edges and filling in the puzzle, a beautiful thing will start to happen. You'll find pieces falling into place. More and more of your life will line up with your calling. The way you use your time, talents, and treasure will reflect the impact you want to have on the world. You'll feel like you have momentum. Eventually, you'll see the empty spots in the puzzle diminishing until there's only one left.

Now, you have the freedom to do and live your dream. All you need to do is slot in that final piece. What is it? If you've been paying attention so far, you'll know that one topic has come up in nearly every single chapter. It's the concept of iteration.

When you grow, new challenges arise. As you fill in the puzzle, you'll find the puzzle changing on you. Remember the airport exercise? Say you reach that five-year vision for your life. What now? It's not as though your life will freeze in place. Things change. If you're living exactly the life you wanted in five years' time, then it's time to paint the picture again, to dream once more.

New constraints, life events, obstacles, and dreams will come up in your life. Don't be afraid to pick up the paintbrush and craft a new vision for yourself. This doesn't mean you're starting over. You get to keep all the gains you've made throughout the process and build on them. The heights you've reached become your new ground floor, holding you up as you climb higher.

Peder and Alison Aadahl 2: How It's Going

Sometimes, you just can't do it all. I remember when we first hired an assistant to help us run the day-to-day operations, and it changed everything. It allowed Peder to stay with us during family vacations and not worry that the business would crumble. This also highlighted how, when it's just you and your spouse working through something, you can get into "A or B" thinking. You want to buy something and he doesn't. Only two choices.

But when you involve a new set of eyes, they'll probably see Options C, D, and E that you two never thought of. Since we hired a coach, we've avoided "A or B" thinking and come up with better ideas than ever. Above all, God will always provide exactly what you need to grow closer to Him and to each other

The Final Piece of the Puzzle? Iteration

The puzzle doesn't ever end. Once you reach the finish line, a new race begins. I know this can feel frustrating for some, especially those who like results. Thankfully, the results you've gained so far are still there. You simply have the opportunity to get more. You've heard it said that life is a journey, not a destination. The same goes for our puzzle. We spend our entire lives unraveling our calling and working to create a ripple effect in the world around us. If we ever "arrived" with a complete puzzle, we'd get bored and stagnant. We're always meant to have a goal to pursue. It always feels like we're moving closer and closer while we build on our tools and discipline.

So, as we master all the previous strategies and tools, we need to add in the practice of checking in with ourselves. I like to do this every year. I sit down with myself and answer questions about where I'm at.

How am I doing with time? Am I investing it to the fullest in the areas I need? Do I have the right spread between work, marriage, family, faith, physical health, and self-improvement, or do I need to make adjustments?

How am I doing with my talents? I evaluate whether I've grown in the skills I need for my journey. I continue to work toward mastery in the most important areas and also identify whether I need any new skills. Lastly, I ask myself whether I'm investing these talents into the proper outlets to see an impact.

Finally, I take a look at treasures. Is there a fresh way I can leverage my calling to make money to take care of my wants and needs? Do I give cheerfully and sacrificially toward causes that matter? Am I doing a good job of being reasonable, not rational, and stewarding my finances well?

This gives me an idea of what I'm doing well, and what needs to improve. It forms the backdrop for the fun question.

What Do You Want to Be When You Grow Up?

We get asked this question as children quite frequently—sometimes, so adults can be entertained by our outlandish responses. We also get asked this question in different forms when we get close to graduating from high school. However, I think we should keep asking this question our whole lives, and never be afraid of it.

You could be 16, 61, or 106 years old. As long as you're still breathing, there's more you're called to do. You can add new elements to your picture, or reinvent it completely. As you go through this entire process, you'll find the whole puzzle growing in its beauty, and possibly, its complexity.

As we go through our lives, the puzzle might go from five hundred pieces to one thousand pieces. Life is relatively simple when we're teenagers. However, complexity grows as we look at careers, marriage, property, children, and retirement. We grow in our capacity to handle the increase of complexity as we go. However, as we get older, we might want to trim it back.

My mom is going through this process right now. She was born in the 1940s. She's been through quite a few different phases in her life, and she has assembled many puzzles. Today, not only her kids but her grandchildren are grown up. Instead of adding complexity, she's looking at things to get rid of, to make it simpler. This is the right move for her phase of life and calling.

The iterations you make don't have to be a certain size. I'm not encouraging you to make only tiny changes or only sweeping reiterations. I'm encouraging you to consistently reexamine what you want the next five years to look like, then pursue it wholeheartedly.

Stick to Five Years

You might ask me why I've consistently asked you to think in terms of five years. That's a fair question. Honestly, the number five doesn't have anything magical about it. I've simply found that it's a happy medium between the long term and the short term.

Anything more than five years seems meaningless in my experience. Like predicting the weather, the further out you go, the more chaotic it gets. It's almost impossible to say with certainty what you'll experience over the next decade. This makes it tough to paint an accurate picture and move toward it.

You'll see this concept when you talk to working-age people about retirement. "What are you going to do when you retire?" you might ask. The answer will probably be, "Travel the world!" That's a fine answer, but it's not a clear picture. Where will they go? When will they go there? How long? Do they even know what age they will be when they retire, or their financial situation, or their health? It's tough to get that specific while planning so far out.

Of course, going shorter presents its own challenges. I think one can reinvent their career and calling in the span of five years; I've done it myself. But if, at the start of my journey, you asked me about my one-year plan instead of five, I would have gotten discouraged. At the end of one year, I was still working my old job! It wasn't until after that year that I moved into a new occupation.

If your new puzzle requires you to get a degree, learn a language, or save up a huge chunk of money, then making a one- or two-year plan probably isn't enough time. You may find yourself in the middle of the process. However, most education and skills can be acquired within three to five years. So, that's the window I stick to. Feel free to experiment with your own ideas on this, though. Depending on your personality, you may find something else working better.

My Five-Year Plan Worked

> God has always provided for us in many ways.
> It's wild to think about how far we've come.
> **—Peder and Alison Aadahl**

The final reason I recommend both five years and iterating is because it worked for me. As I've mentioned, I left a corporate job and started my own business that helps teach men about Inspired Living. It took some planning on the front end, then a full year of working a job I didn't enjoy and saving every penny I could.

But finally, I made the transition back in 2017. I started my own business and worked hard to build it into something I was proud of. Today, not everything is perfect, but by and large, I've managed to assemble my puzzle. If I ran into an old friend at the airport today, I'd get to tell them all the reasons my life is fantastic:

- Instead of working long days at an office somewhere, I get to build my own schedule and work where I want. This means that most days, I get to eat lunch with my wife. There is no overinvestment in work and underinvestment in marriage. This is one of the primary reasons I wanted to make a change, and one of the reasons my wife supported me from the start.

- Speaking of building my own schedule, I recently got to drop everything and take half a day off. I drove to Texas A&M San Antonio and put an Aggie Ring on my bonus daughter. Assembling my puzzle meant I could be there for a milestone moment in her life.

- As my son has grown into an adult, I remember days when I got to focus less on work and more on helping him find an apartment. Instead of saying, "My dad makes a bunch of money, but he's never really here," I want my son to say, "My dad always has time for me."

All these are things I'd never be able to do in my corporate job. Now, don't get me wrong, there's some sacrifice involved. I made more money then; quite a bit more. However, I'm happier today. What do we gain if we profit the world but lose our souls?

As I look back over the past several years, I see that I'm living my puzzle. Now, I don't want to sit back and rest on my laurels. I want to assemble a new puzzle. I've seen the fruits that come from following this process, and I want to apply it to a new set of challenges. My season in life is changing as my kids move out and become less and less dependent on us. I've gained a career's worth of knowledge and experience. Now, I want to invest in a business that totally feels like what I've been put on this planet to do.

That's what it comes down to. When we start figuring out our calling, we get meaning and purpose. We understand why we've been put on this earth. That's an incredibly empowering feeling, one I wouldn't trade for any amount of cash. When you know what you've been put on this planet for, you can joyfully and confidently live out your calling and leave a lasting impact on the world. Now that's what I call Inspired Living.

You can do this too. I pray that you take everything we've gone over in this book so far and work it into your life. Adapt all the strategies and tools I've shared to your unique personality. Align your time, talents, and treasure in a way that enables you to influence others and leave a ripple effect on this world. You have no idea the kind of impact you can have through stewarding your life in this way.

Lastly, I encourage you to get started right away. Soon, you'll close this book and go back to your regularly scheduled programming. It's easy to let these lessons and inspiration slip away and let this be another "shelf help" book that collects dust in your office or living room. I don't want that to be your story, and I reckon you don't either. Find a way to start the process this very week. Begin investing in yourself immediately. I can't wait to see the kind of puzzle you put together.

Chapter Summary

No puzzle lasts forever. As you follow this process, you'll find yourself becoming the person you envision. Your life will slowly align with the picture you painted. Now, it's time to iterate. That's the final piece of the puzzle. Instead of remaining frozen in time, build a new puzzle! I do this every five years, which gives me enough time to complete something meaningful, but not so much that my prediction loses accuracy.

The reason I believe so much in this process is because it works for me. I was able to leave my old job and line up my job, relationships, and finances with my calling. Every day I wake up glad that I have the job I have, and closer to my wife and kids than ever before. I can't wait to see what the next puzzle has in store for me.

Key Takeaways

- Now that you've worked the edges and find yourself filling in the middle, keep going! Learn from feedback and keep plugging away until the last few pieces remain.
- As you complete each puzzle, ask yourself what you want to be when you grow up. Don't be afraid to paint a new picture and build a new puzzle.
- Pay close attention to the things you do that make you feel like you've found your purpose.

Conclusion and Invitation

You made it.

Thank you so much for reading all the way to the end. As somebody who has found a passion in helping people discover their calling and develop their influence on the world, it blesses me that you would take the time to invest in yourself like this. I hope that what we've covered in this book helps you with just that. I want to leave you with a few reminders about what we've discussed, and then leave you with an invitation.

The first section of this book was all about discovering how to live out your calling. We began by examining how we can invest in ourselves because that's where it all begins. This includes our mindset, habits, and the time we give to invest in ourselves. Then, we expanded outward into investing in others. The primary currency for this investment is time. As you invest in others, you'll start to see certain themes and patterns resonate. This points you in the direction of your calling.

As you invest in others over time, you begin to develop an influence on people. Even if it starts small, with just one person, you can begin making a difference. This work further narrows your calling down as you get a better read on the activities that give you life and deliver positive results. As you go along this path, you begin to have an impact on the world. This ripples out far beyond our own lifetimes, but all we need to worry about is the next step right in front of us.

In the second section, we got more practical. We talked about the main pieces needed to live out our calling, which are the way we steward our time, talents, and treasures. Leveraging these three items toward a positive vision amplifies our impact. In the chapter about time, I talked about the interplay between managing our time, our energy, and our focus. We also discussed how to get the most out of productivity tools, even if we aren't the most conscientious personality.

This also introduced the iterative process: plan, execute, review, revise, and repeat. This process acts like a science experiment, giving us data on the methods that work best for our context and personality. This process came into play for the rest of the book.

In talents, I explained that most coaching issues are presented as time or treasure problems, but they actually come down to a talent problem in reality. If we hone the right skills, and apply them correctly, we'll find ourselves with more time and more money as we go. This requires extremely honest self-examination and more iterations.

In treasures, we discussed the importance of being reasonable, not rational. Humans aren't robots, and thus we need a more organic approach to money than something simply mathematical. To steward our money better, we need to connect our "why" to our money and avoid making drastic changes. Instead of taking advantage of compound interest like so many gurus advise us, we should instead focus on compound behavior.

Finally, the third section was all about putting everything together. We began by getting a vision of our future using the airport question, which examines what we want our life to look like in five years. This allowed us to identify the main pieces of our puzzle and the main constraints we had to work with. Using this vision, we "worked the edges," coming up with answers to five crucial questions about our tasks and behaviors.

Then, we filled in the middle. With an understanding of what we should be doing, and what we shouldn't be doing, we made it as easy as possible to do the former and added friction to avoid doing the latter. It's simple, but far from easy. In fact, the ability to consistently do what you should and not do what you shouldn't separates the extremely successful people from the rest of the population. So, we need to leverage every system for accountability, inspiration, habituation, and productivity we can.

Last of all, we looked at the final piece of the puzzle: iteration. When you assemble your first puzzle, you get the opportunity to build another one. I left you with encouragement to never stop dreaming about what you want to be when you grow up, to continue making five-year plans, and to keep unraveling your calling and impact on the world. Through repeating this process, your life embodies Inspired Living.

Now, it's up to you. I did my best to give you all the wisdom and tools I could to make the process simple for you. I explained how I followed this process in my own life to assemble a life I love. I sprinkled in stories of other people who have done the same. However, you can lead a horse to water, but you can't make them drink.

It's time for you to get started. By now, you've probably done a couple of the exercises listed in the book, or at least thought about your answers to some of the questions I've posed. But only you can keep going, day in and day out, as you put together your puzzle. Will you join the happy few people seeking to live out their calling to the fullest? If so, you'll be in good company.

If you need guidance and support, I'm here to help. Just visit InspiredLivingBook.com to find helpful resources and many ways you can connect with me directly.

Acknowledgments

Writing a book is way harder than it has any right to be and way more rewarding as well. None of this would have been possible at all without the great support of my wife, Carrie. She was the first person to tell me that I should "finally write that book I've been talking about" and "well if you can't do it alone, what would you tell someone else to do? Get some help."

I'm also fortunate to have been surrounded by my son David, daughter Glory, and my God daughters. They don't always understand why I wanted to make this book happen but they've offered their love and support throughout the process since they love and support me.

I'd love to thank Dan Miller, not just for writing my foreword but for being a great virtual mentor for decades of my life. Without his group, the 48 Days Eagles, and hearing his voice in my head saying "You can do this" I wouldn't have ever set down and put this book together.

All those who I interviewed are also friends and mentors.

Marcus wrote his own great book on Stewardship and has gifted me his time multiple times to help me when I have questions. He's one of the most generous men I know.

Wade's ability to find ways to help people master their time is one that I've learned from observing from afar and he's always been kind sharing that knowledge, and his precious time, with me.

Tim is a friend and someone who I've learned tons from when it comes to business and marketing. He's also a client but I've learned as much from him as he has from me.

I'm one of Jeff's true fans. He helped me start my podcast where many of the ideas in this book were first thought about and talked about. He also introduced me to many others through his mastermind and podcast, *Read to Lead*.

Stephanie is a master marketer and event planner. I've observed her from afar and learned much from her but, again, like so many others, she's been generous with her time and knowledge.

Aaron is another virtual mentor who I've learned a ton from on how to support and mentor others. His writing and videos have helped me often when I am not believing in myself.

Chris is another virtual mentor. He's taught me a ton about DISC and how to use that knowledge to help me be a better coach, but more importantly a better person.

Darryl is one of the most "hidden gems" in my local area. He's mentored tons of people and never toots his own horn, but I've learned a ton about serving others well by observing him.

Peder and Alison are not only my clients but I also consider them friends. I'd like to thank them for allowing me to share just a small part of their story and journey with all of you in this book. I've had the pleasure of working with a number of awesome clients over the years but Peder and Alison are something special. Their willingness to be vulnerable and transparent allowed me to highlight their journey throughout the book and I'll be forever grateful for their willingness to share and support on this journey.

That brings me to the biggest help I had, Nick. He told me I didn't have to mention him but I'd be remiss not to. He is a friend first but he also went out of his way to help me with all steps of the process throughout. This book would never have happened without his support and guidance.

I'd also love to thank my editor, Catherine. Any errors that remain are certainly mine, but I promise you there would be many more without her careful work and great eye.

I'd like to also thank the great team over at Morgan James Publishing who not only helped with support and guidance but made me feel welcome indeed. This includes Addy, first and foremost who was the point of contact that kept me on schedule and made sure I didn't miss any of the things I had to do to make this book come to your hands. Naomi made we feel welcome right away. And David and Jim also offered their advice and support throughout the process.

About the Author

Scott Maderer loves to help people really live out their calling by helping them master their time, talent, and treasures so they can really find and focus on their calling.

Scott was a school teacher for sixteen years, teaching science from grades 6 to 12 in Texas. Later, according to his students, he joined the dark side and began working in the educational testing industry for eleven years including serving in senior leadership.

In 2011, Scott and his wife, Carrie, started a coaching business on the side while discovering how to help others master their calling. Their coaching helps clients align the way they use their time, talent, and treasures so they can identify and live a fully authentic life that allows them to authentically live their calling, serve others, and provide for their families.

As certified Human Behavior Senior Consultants and members of the Maxwell Leadership Certified Team, Scott and Carrie focus on helping people understand themselves, understand others, and, through that understanding, build the Kingdom. In 2017, they took the business full-time, offering assistance through one-on-one coaching, speaking, and workshops. Scott has personally worked with clients in fifteen countries and loves his thirty-second commute to work while managing to help clients all over the world.

Scott and Carrie live in the Hill Country outside of San Antonio, Texas, forty-five minutes from the closest Walmart, Starbucks, or McDonald's. But they love it out there. They've successfully raised a great young man who has graduated and doesn't live in their basement. They also love spending time with their bonus daughter and two God daughters as often as they can.

A free ebook edition is available with the purchase of this book.

To claim your free ebook edition:

1. Visit MorganJamesBOGO.com
2. Sign your name CLEARLY in the space
3. Complete the form and submit a photo of the entire copyright page
4. You or your friend can download the ebook to your preferred device

Print & Digital Together Forever.

Snap a photo

Free ebook

Read anywhere